A
TRAVELLER'S
WINE GUIDE
TO

Italy

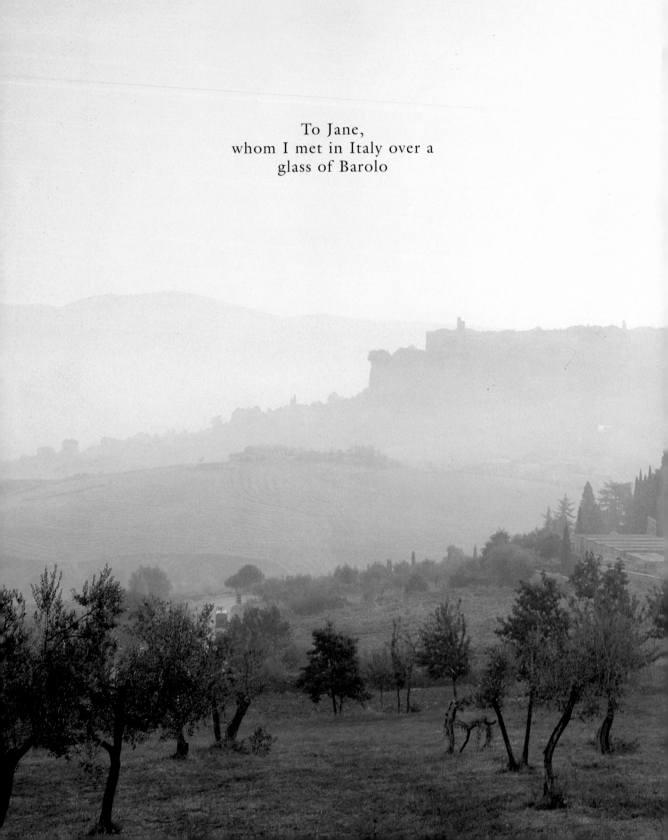

To Jane,
whom I met in Italy over a
glass of Barolo

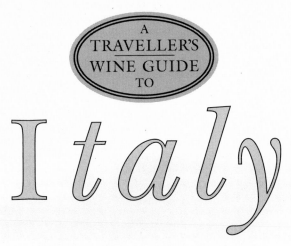

A TRAVELLER'S WINE GUIDE TO

Italy

Stephen Hobley

Foreword by Donatella Cinelli Colombini

Photographs by Francesco Venturi

Aurum Press

The *Traveller's Wine Guides* were conceived and produced by Philip Clark Ltd, 53 Calton Avenue, London SE21 7DF, UK

Designed by Keith Faulkner Publishing Ltd

Edited by Philip Clark and Tony Raven

Photographs by Franceso Venturi (except where otherwise credited)

Maps by European Map Graphics Ltd, Andrew Green and Simon Green

Copyright © Philip Clark Ltd, 1989, 1997

First Edition published in 1989

This revised and updated edition published in 1997 by Aurum Press Ltd, 25 Bedford Avenue, London WC1B 3AT, UK

A catalogue record for this book is available from the British Library.

ISBN 1-85410-456-X

Printed and bound in Hong Kong

ACKNOWLEDGEMENTS

Philip Clark Ltd would particularly like to thank Joanne Doherty for reading the proofs and Tony Raven for his help in editing the text and preparing the index.

The author would like to thank: Roberto Bava for help in contacting his fellow wine producers; Paolo Valdastri for enlightening comments on the Livorno and Pisa section; Giampaolo Pacini for introducing some hidden parts of Tuscany; Ursula Thurner and Donatella Cinelli Colombini for their support and enthusiasm. The wine producers who helped by suggesting sights to visit as well as providing information about their own visiting hours and conditions are too numerous to mention individually, but without them, this book would have been impossible to put together.

COVER
Designed by Janet James

Main illustration: Vines and citrus groves on the cliffs near Amalfi, Campania. (Photograph: Mick Rock/Cephas Picture Library)

Foreground photography by Darius

Road map of Italy: 1:200,000 edited by Touring Club Italiano. Reproduction authorized 23.5.96.

TITLE ILLUSTRATION
The city of Orvieto in Umbria looms through the early morning mist over cypresses and olive trees. Orvieto is sited on a natural fortress of volcanic rock. (Photograph: Alan Williams)

PHOTO CREDITS
Maureen Ashley MW 131
Azienda Agricola Contucci 99
Azienda Agricola San Felice 92
Casa Vinicola Collavini 64
Casa Vinicola Umberto Fiore 30
Casa Vinicola Roberto Kechler von Schwandorf 71
Co-operativa Locorotondo 117
Co-operativa Monte Schiavo 110
Italian Trade Centre, London 78
C. Penna (Bava Collection) 14, 25
Mick Rock/Cephas Picture Library 124-5
Alan Williams 22, 33, 35, 41, 56, 57, 84/85, 76, 77, 79, 89, 101, 126, 130, 132
Zefa Picture Library 38/39, 44

Contents

How to Use this Book

This book is a starting point. It provides a wealth of information on Italian wine, some reflections on cultural and gastronomic points of interest in Italy, and some suggested itineraries for visiting selected wineries. Its unique advantage over other books on Italian wine is that it gives so much practical information about whom to visit and what to expect when you get there.

To get the best use out of this book, you need:
a) a good set of maps. The most useful are the 1:200,000 series produced by the Touring Club of Italy, the TCI.
b) to plan ahead. Wine tourism is a relatively new concept in Italy and many of the producers listed in this book have said that they preferred advance booking by telephone or fax.

Remember, however, that these are guidelines rather than rules. This is Italy. It may not be necessary to book every visit. Enthusiasm and a smile on the part of the visitor wins round all but the most hardened or hard-pressed Italian. There is always an element of serendipity in any unplanned meeting for winemaker and visitor alike.

Equally, many producers have stated that there is a charge for tasting. This is not a rigid law either. It makes sense to charge organized groups for a tasting. In that way, everyone knows where they stand, and local cheeses and salami are often part of the package too. But individual wine enthusiasts can build a rapport with the winemaker that goes beyond the strictly commercial.

Booking ahead
Advance booking by fax is easier (see page 141 for suggested wording). Areas used to general tourism, such as Tuscany and the Veneto, have a long tradition of winery-gate sales to the general public anyway.

However, it is undoubtedly true that you will receive a better tour of the winery if you telephone or fax in advance, especially if your visit is to involve more than just purchasing wine.

The itineraries in this book are, of course, in no way obligatory, and deviation from the sequence of visits suggested does not matter at all.

The main text describes areas to go to – for example the Langhe in Piedmont, the Franciacorta in Lombardy, and Chianti Classico in Tuscany – rather than individual wine producers to visit (except where the producer is exceptionally important or where space has permitted).

The blue information panels
More often, the information about individual wine producers, wine shops and wine exhibitions is to be found in the blue information panels by the side of the main text. All the producers – and shops – detailed in these panels are recommended for the quality of their wines, but the list is, of course, by no means fully comprehensive.

The panels will provide you with information which should be helpful when visiting a winery. The symbols used (see the explanatory panel, right) let you know what to expect.

Most wine companies offer tours on the tacit assumption that a small purchase at least will be made. Visits to a winery (see pages 12-13) can be an education and a great pleasure; a real interest is always rewarded.

Wine to be tasted will vary from the honestly cheap and cheerful to the expensive and carefully crafted.

Just like any other businesses, wineries are usually open during office hours only. Most of them are closed on Sundays, in the month of August, and between Christmas and the New Year.

INFORMATION PANEL
SYMBOLS

E	English spoken
F	French spoken
G	German spoken
S	Spanish spoken
TF	free wine-tasting offered
TP	paid-for wine-tasting
WS	wine for sale
B	booking required
b	booking advisable

EP   *Enoteca pubblica* local government-sponsored wine exhibition centre, sometimes including museum and restaurant
ER   *Enoteca regionale* regional wine exhibition centre, the most important type of *Enoteca pubblica*
*   Member of *Movimento del Turismo del Vino* (see below)

MOVIMENTO DEL TURISMO DEL VINO
The national Movement for Wine Tourism in Italy is run by wine producers, and has as its aim the development of wine tourism to the mutual benefit of visitors and producers alike. It is responsible for the rapid development of the popularity of wine tourism in Italy, especially in Tuscany, Piedmont and Emilia-Romagna.

Fax: 0577 849356.

Foreword

by Donatella Cinelli Colombini, President of the *Movimento del Turismo del Vino*

This book takes you to vineyards that look like gardens, with roses planted at the end of each row of vines; to wineries with their own museums attached; to cellars beneath Renaissance villas; to castles and to entire medieval hamlets with wine barrels in place of inhabitants. So many wonderful wines, all with their own story to tell.

Stephen Hobley shares with you his experience of the places where great Italian wines are made; very few people can help the traveller to understand these areas as he can. Learning about them is a rewarding task: just look carefully at the gently rolling hills where the vines grow, at the cellars with their wine casks, and listen to the producers and the cellarmasters who welcome you. Many of the smaller producers will press you to taste their wines in their own homes. In Italy, whoever goes into a cellar as a potential customer leaves it as a friend.

The wine traveller does not have to be an expert. It is enough to have some enthusiasm for the subject, to love being in the country, and to have just a little spirit of adventure. Some of the places recommended in this book are as yet unused to wine tourism and to some extent you will be a pioneer.

This book takes you to places where the scenery seems to come straight out of a Renaissance painting, where you eat and drink well, often at a very reasonable cost. Wine tourism can be integrated into a traditional holiday in Italy, and combined with a visit to Florence, Venice, Rome or the Mediterranean resorts. It is enough to remember that in the Uffizi Gallery you are less than an hour away by car from a producer in the courtyard of whose castle you will be able to taste wine while admiring the bas-relief by Donatello.

After the crush of the alleys and piazzas of Venice, it is a relief to visit a villa designed by the great architect Sanmicheli and surrounded by vineyards that produce an excellent white wine. Those who like archaeology can admire the Forum or the Colosseum, but there are also wine cellars built out of old Roman cisterns and at least one vinification tank carved out of stone over two thousand years ago. Wine tourism gives you the opportunity to enhance your holiday in Italy with something new, something a bit different and a pleasure at the same time.

When you return home and invite your friends to dinner, you will be able to serve wine bought in Italy and tell your guests: 'This is one of my discoveries; it comes from a Tuscan villa that has a collection of rare farm animals that the owner is trying to save from extinction.' What you need not explain is that the wine cost you less than a bottle of table wine from your local shop. This must be one of the secrets closely guarded between you, a pioneer of wine tourism, and the wine producers of Italy.

Donatella Cinelli Colombini

Introduction

Italy has never lacked style. Lamborghini and Ferrari, Gucci and Armani – these are all internationally revered names. The Italian sense of style and the Italian way of living are generally much admired. And Italian food and the Mediterranean diet have made an impact worldwide. To many foreigners, however, Italian wine is just something to drink with spaghetti or pizza at home. It is difficult to understand in a world enamoured of the simple tastes of Chardonnay, Cabernet and oak.

But, as the Californians are starting to say, 'ABC – Anything But Chardonnay', meaning 'I shall die of boredom if I have to drink another full oak Chardonnay.' Anyone who holds any prejudices about Italian wines is in danger of missing out on a whole glorious new world of tastes, from superb native Italian grapes, such as Sangiovese (in Chianti, Vino Nobile di Montepulciano, and Brunello di Montalcino) and Nebbiolo (in Barolo), to new interpretations of the classic international grapes (Chardonnay, Cabernet, Pinot Noir and Sauvignon).

Over one million hectares of vineyards produce about 70 million hectolitres of wine in Italy per year. (That is over 1500 million imperial, and over 1800 US gallons.) The province of Trapani in Sicily alone makes more wine per annum than the whole of Australia.

In Italy, wine is more than a drink. It is also part of the geography, history and general culture of the country. Perhaps there is no other country in the world where wine tourism and gastronomic tourism are so varied.

Each region, every town even, has its own wines and foods, a variety of preparations that have been handed down from generation to generation, so that, just as there is no such thing as Italian Food, there is no such thing as Italian Wine. It is all regional.

Regional does not, however, mean provincial. Just like every other country in the Old Wine World, Italy is busy re-examining its local heritage at the same moment as it is assessing the new possibilities brought by internationally

successful grapes as well as production methods – principally, maturation in the small French new oak *barrique* (cask) rather than the traditional large old Slavonian oak barrel. Wine producers realise that both export and education are vitally important.

This is where the wine tourist comes in – you. Be assured of your welcome in Italy. The Italians are naturally hospitable, but they are also well aware that the long-term future of Italian wine is bound up in the communication of the pleasures of the Italian table, food and wine, to an audience.

Look out for the current bandwagons: ageing in *barriques* – this lends a vanilla taste to the wine and makes it more 'international'; the rediscovery of local grape varieties; the introduction of international grape varieties – Cabernet Sauvignon and Chardonnay, for example; and the increase in sales of sparkling wine.

There has never been a more exciting time to discover Italian wine.

Bolzano

FRIULI-
VENEZIA
GIULIA

NORTH
CENTRAL
ITALY
Trento

VENETO
Venice

Trieste

Aosta

NORTH-
WEST
ITALY
Milan

Verona

Turin

Genoa

VIA EMILIA
Bologna

ADRIATIC
SEA

Florence

Pisa

TUSCANY

Ancona

Siena

Perugia

CENTRAL
ITALY

Pescara

l'Aquila

Rome

Campobasso

ADRIATIC
COAST

SARDINIA

Naples
Potenza

Bari

Taranto
Lecce

MEDITERRANEAN
COAST

TYRRHENIAN
SEA

Cagliari

Catanzaro

Messina

Palermo

SICILY

Pantelleria

The Classification of Wines

1990 *the vintage*

1990

Vigneto Antica Chiusina *vineyard name. This wine is from a single, and therefore by implication superior, vineyard*

L3215 *bottling batch number*

Imbottigliato all'origine … *estate bottled by …* **Saiagricola** *name of company that owns the estate* **SPA** *Limited Company (Ltd/Inc.)*

13% *alcoholic strength. A high level of alcohol indicates a serious wine (11% or 12% is more normal)*

Fattoria del Cerro *the producer's name*

VIGNETO **ANTICA CHIUSINA** *VINO NOBILE DI MONTEPULCIANO* DENOMINAZIONE DI ORIGINE CONTROLLATA E GARANTITA

FATTORIA DEL CERRO IMBOTTIGLIATO ALL'ORIGINE DA S.P.A SAIAGRICOLA PRODUTTORE IN MONTEPULCIANO · ITALIA

13% vol.   750 ml e

Vino Nobile di Montepulciano *the type of wine*

Denominazione di Origine Controllata e Garantita *DOCG, the highest quality classification*

Produttore in Montepulciano, Italia *producer in Montepulciano, Italy (i.e. not a négociant-bottler, but a producer owning vineyards in the wine production area)*

750 ml *bottle size (three-quarters of a litre). The standard size is 75cl for quality wine, one litre for ordinary table wine.*

Non disperdere il vetro nell'ambiente *statutory exhortation to dispose of the bottle carefully*

Reading the label

Ultimately, the producer's name is always a more reliable guarantee of quality than any official qualification on the label, but knowledge of a few basic terms helps in predicting what a wine should be like. As more and more wines are brought into the official DOC system, the days when it seemed that Italy's best and worst wines were labelled *vino da tavola* are coming to an end, and labels are beginning to mean more.

(DOCG) Denominazione di Origine Controllata e Garantita

The top classification and the one with most significance for quality as well as for tipicity. Independent tasting commissions verify the quality of wine at this level and relatively few wines are included.

The reds are: Barbaresco, Barolo, and Gattinara from Piedmont; Brunello di Montalcino, Carmignano, Chianti, and Vino Nobile di Montepulciano from Tuscany; Montefalco Sagrantino and Torgiano Riserva from Umbria; and Taurasi from Campania.

The whites are: Albana di Romagna from Emilia-Romagna, Moscato d'Asti and Asti (formerly Asti Spumante) from Piedmont, and Vernaccia di San Gimignano from Tuscany. There is one bottle-fermented sparkling DOCG wine: Franciacorta from Lombardy.

DOC (Denominazione di Origine Controllata)

The cornerstone of the Italian system, DOC regulations set maximum yields from the vineyards, maximum yields in terms of must from the grapes, minimum alcohol levels, and precise

COLLIO

C 017051 1
CONTROLLO DELLA QUALITÀ
INCARICO VIGILANZA DM. 26.11.1975
CONSORZIO TUTELA VINI
COLLIO VQPRD

geographic origins. Entire regions can have umbrella DOC's (Piedmont is the most important) and tiny areas can have their own denomination (Loazzolo in Piedmont is Italy's smallest DOC, with only five producers).

IGT (Indicazione Geografica Tipica)

Similar to French *vin de pays*. The first wines in this category appeared only in 1996. This is the base of the Italian wine quality pyramid, whose apex is DOCG and whose middle is DOC.

Vino da Tavola

This includes any wine that does not fall into the quality categories above. In the past the very best of Italian wines (Solaia, see right, for example) and the very worst wines have both been designated *Vino da Tavola*, the best wines because they did not use prescribed grapes or prescribed methods of production, the worst wines because they lacked quality. The top wines are now being brought into the DOC/G system, but there will be a transitional stage over several years when *Vino da Tavola* remains ambiguous, in theory. In practice, there is no confusion; price and presentation see to that.

Types of producers

Tenuta, Castello, Podere, Fattoria: traditional agricultural estates more or less devoted to wine production.

Azienda Agricola: a wine estate producing its own grapes. It will generally consider itself superior to the following:

Casa Vinicola: wine-makers using bought-in grapes. They will argue that by buying in grapes they control what they get with greater accuracy.

Co-operativa: a co-operative.

Solaia (top) is an upmarket wine made by Antinori, a leading Italian producer, but it still ranks as a Vino da Tavola. VIDE (above left) is a voluntary quality control association label that gives its authorization to approved wines. Vigneti Casterna (centre left) is a DOC wine, a single-vineyard Valpolicella.

Neck labels with Consorzio symbols (below) are issued by the Consorzios to indicate that a wine has met with their minimum standards of wine production.

Basic wine terms

Bianco, Rosso, Rosato red, white, rosé

Classico from the heartland of the traditional production area. By implication (and usually in fact) better than others in the region.

Superiore with slightly higher alcohol and, for reds, aged longer.

Riserva aged longer and therefore necessarily of higher quality.

Spumante sparkling wine, usually made in the cheaper tank method rather than bottle-fermented.

Talento generic term for all bottle-fermented sparkling wines (except Franciacorta).

Vigna single vineyard.

Vino biologico organic wine.

Vino novello new wine, to be drunk as young as possible, as with French Beaujolais Nouveau.

Visiting a Winery

This book is not intended to encourage drinking and driving in any way. Italian law is rightly strict in its sanctions against motorists who offend in this respect. To help your motoring to be worry-free, here are a few useful points to bear in mind:

Speed limits
In town: 50km/h (31 mph)
Out of town: 90km/h (55 mph)
Motorways: 130km/h (81 mph)

Alcohol limit: 80mg per 100ml of blood

Motorway tolls
About 80 lire per km

Motoring tips
• Service stations are usually closed during the lunch hour (longer in summer) and all day on Sunday. Exceptions are the 24hr motorway services and the automatic cash machine pumps on some forecourts (uncrumpled 10,000 lire notes are essential).
• Always pay cash for fuel.
• Illegal parking in Rome can carry a prison sentence.
• Stick to motorways for longer distances; local roads are invariably congested except in deep country.
• Traffic police can demand heavy on-the-spot fines for speeding.
• Carry your driving licence and passport with you at all times.

The vineleaf insignia of the Associazione Enotecnici Italiani (Italian Association of Wine Technicians). The AEI are experts on the technical analysis of wine.

Booking a visit

Most wineries require some notice of an impending visit, for practical reasons. *In extremis*, however, if you arrive without warning and express interest, you will find Italians never less than courteous and always willing to help you if possible.

Booking can be made by fax, telephone or letter (see page 141 for a sample fax/letter in Italian). It is sometimes sufficient to express interest, but most wineries accept visitors on the understanding that some purchase will be made, however small.

Types of visit

Co-operatives These vary considerably in size and outlook. In general, it is those that are proud of their wines, and keen to show that being a co-operative is no handicap to making good wines, that are most ready to welcome foreign visitors.

Some co-operatives, however, concentrate solely on bulk wine for local consumption and are less interested in visitors.

Large private companies The grandest companies, the Antinoris and Ruffinos of the Italian wine world, have public relations departments, but these are not generally orientated towards the public. When arranging your visits, it is often best to contact the individual winery rather than depend on the main office.

Small private companies These are often the most rewarding to visit. The wine producer is often also the owner of the company, although he will probably have a consultant wine expert (an enologist) for the technical aspects of wine-making. Many producers are total enthusiasts who are dedicated to promoting their wines. Like most enthusiasts, they are fascinating to talk to on their subject.

Enoteche Enoteche means 'places of wine'. Two types are mentioned in this book (see page 6).
1. 'Public Exhibition and/or Tasting Centre' – usually run by local government. The general purpose is educational. Booking may be necessary for a guided tour.
2. The equivalent of a 'Specialist Wine Shop' – a commercial enterprise. Like any shop, booking is not necessary and tasting is not usually offered, although if the shop doubles as a wine bar it will, of course, provide wine by the glass and at least a range of snack food.

Tasting wine

It is very helpful to take notes when you taste wine, so that you can build up a sort of reference system, and thus more easily compare one wine with another tasted some time before. It is useful to examine at least three aspects of the wine:

Colour A light white is lighter in colour than a heavier white. A young red is brighter than an older red.

Nose Much of the taste of a wine can be predicted from its smell. The perfume of the wine itself is part of the sensory pleasure of drinking. Tasters differentiate between the primary aromas of fruit from the grapes or wood from the barrel and the secondary aromas of the mature, fully integrated, wine.

Taste Does the wine balance the taste of the grape with the tannin (in red wines) or with the alcohol and the acidity? Is there a particular aftertaste to the wine?

Don't forget though that wine is to be enjoyed. If you like it, say so, and try to find a reason why.

If not, the reason why you didn't like it is equally important.

The process of wine-making

White wines

1. White (or red) grapes are broken away from their stems by machine.
2. A press crushes the grapes to extract the juice. This is separated from the skins and pumped into a fermentation vat (usually of stainless steel, and equipped for temperature control).
3. Fermentation ends. Sweet wine results when it is stopped before all the sugar in the grapes turns into alcohol. Vice-versa for dry wine.
4. When fermentation is complete and the wine has been drained (racked) off the sediment (lees) and clarified (fined), it is stored in large vats (often made of glass-lined concrete) until bottling.

Red wines

1. After crushing and de-stemming, the grapes are put into a vat to ferment.
2. Fermentation lasts until the sugar is used up, about a fortnight.
3. Racking and fining, as for white wines, above.
4. The wine is aged: in stainless steel for light wine, large barrels for a heavier wine, small barrels (*barriques*) for special wines that require the vanilla flavours of wood.

Sparkling wines

The process of fermentation usually provides the bubbles. The most expensive and prestigious way of doing this is to give the wine a natural second fermentation in the bottle itself in what used to be described as the 'Champagne method', but now has to be called simply 'bottle-fermentation'. Italians sometimes call this the *metodo classico*, or *metodo tradizionale*.

Less expensive is the 'Charmat' or tank method, which uses a single stainless steel fermentation vat to induce bubbles in the wine, a whole tankful at a time.

Really cheap sparkling wine is produced by adding carbon dioxide to an ordinary wine, just like the bubbles in most mineral water.

Price is a good rule of thumb with sparkling wine, but such is the confusion in the Italian sparkling wine industry that the generic word *spumante*, sparkling wine, has acquired negative connotations.

The extent of this trend is indicated by the fact that Asti Spumante – now DOCG (see page 10) has dropped the 'Spumante' from its name.

TASTING WINE – THE BASICS

1. *Hold the glass to the light to assess the wine's colour.*

2. *Smell the wine.*

3. *Swirl the wine in the glass to liberate the flavour.*

4. *Sip the wine and move it around inside your mouth.*

5. *Spitting accurately is not easy. (Practise beforehand with a glass of water!)*

13

North-West Italy

Orth-west Italy comprises two areas of lesser importance in wine terms, Valle d'Aosta and Liguria, and one area which produces some of the finest wines in the world – Piedmont. Valle d'Aosta and Liguria are both mountainous areas, and they present extreme difficulties for the cultivation of vineyards. Wine in the Valle d'Aosta is produced with enormous effort from steeply sloping terraces which are clearly visible on both sides of the narrow Dora Baltea valley.

Similarly, in Liguria, a boat trip around the headlands of the Cinque Terre or east of Savona towards the French border will reveal yet more precipitous vineyards in more hand-cultivated terraces. Unfortunately, the wines of both areas tend to be relatively expensive, precisely because of these difficulties of production. But wine quality continues to rise in both regions despite a dramatic decline in viticulture in the last few years.

Fields and vineyards near the wine town of Asti create geometric patterns in shades of green.

Each of the three regions has a distinct character. The Aostans have always regarded themselves as an independent mountain people, while the Ligurians have a proud seafaring heritage that goes back to the Genoese trade empire in the Middle Ages. But it was the Piedmontese who unified Italy, under King Victor Emmanuel (from 1861), and who still view the results with a somewhat amused detachment.

Piedmont is the Burgundy of Italy. It has a proud ducal past, its wines are produced on innumerable smallholdings according to ancient traditions, and few people claim to understand the *cru* (single vineyard) nature of its most famous wines, Barolo and Barbaresco. But even a lowly trattoria will produce a very drinkable opaque wine, normally one of the house reds: Dolcetto and Barbera. Their characteristic slight *pétillance* is not a sign of bad winemaking, but rather of how Italians like their young red wines. The major change in recent years is the rise to importance of white wines, Chardonnay particularly, as well as the more local Gavi, Erbaluce, Favorita and Arneis.

Also included in this section is a part of Lombardy, the sparkling wine producing area of Oltrepò Pavese.

PRINCIPAL VINEYARD AREAS

- Aosta wines
- Erbaluce di Caluso
- Oltrepò Pavese
- Barolo
- Barbaresco
- Asti and Moscato d'Asti
- Gavi and Cortese di Gavi
- Rossese di Dolceacqua
- Cinque Terre

Domodóssola

R. Dora Baltea
Courmayeur
Morgex
La Salle   Quart Nus
Arvier   Aosta   Chambave
Amavilles   Fenis   SS26
R. Sesia
Varese

Arnaz
Donnas   Gattinara
Carema   Biella
Ivrea   Ghemme Fara
L. Viverone
SS299
A8
A4
SS11
Milan

R. Orco
A5
Novara
R. Ticino
SS35
SS25
A26   Vercelli
R. Po   SS31
R. Agogna   Pavia
A7   R. Po
Turin
Chieri   Castelnuovo Don Bosco
Sestriere   SS10
Pessione   Alessandria   A21
Pinerolo   Tortona
SS23   Poirino
Asti
Canale
R. Po   Sta Vittoria   Costigliole d'Asti
d'Alba   Barbaresco Nizza
Saluzzo   Alba   Canelli
Bra   Gavi
SS20 SS231   Acqui Terme
Barolo   Ovada
SS29
Dogliani
R. Stura di Demonte   A6
Cuneo
R. Tanaro
A10
Genoa
Savona   A12
Portofino   SS1

LIGURIAN SEA

Monterosso
Dolceacqua   La Spezia
Ventimiglia San Remo   Imperia

15

Valle d'Aosta

AOSTA
Institut Agricole
Régional* Reg La Rochère
1/a. Tel: 0165 553304. Fax:
0165 553297. (Luciano
Rigazio). F.TP.WS.B.

AYMAVILLES
Az Agr Les Crêtes* Loc
Villetos 50. Tel: 0165
902274. Fax: 0165 902758.
(Costantino Charrere). 0830-
1200, 1430-1900. Property
includes 18th-century mill
and olive mill. E.F.TP.WS.B.
Cave des Onze
Communes* Fraz Urbains
14. Tel/Fax: 0165 902912
(Dino Darensod). F.TP.WS.B.

CHAMBAVE
La Crotta di Vegnerons*
Piazza Roncas 7 (near Fenis).
Tel/Fax: 0166 46670. (Yves
Burgay, Andrea Costa, Rino
Lillaz). Tue, Wed, Fri 0830-
1200, 1400-1700, Sat 0830-
1200. F.TP.WS.B.

DONNAS
Coop. Caves de Donnas*
Via Roma 97. Tel: 0125
807096. (Giulio Follioley).
F.TP.WS.B.

MORGEX
Coop. Cave du Vin
Blanc de Morgex et La
Salle* Loc Les Iles. Tel:
0165 800331. Fax: 0165
800401. (Corrado Chatel).
F.TP.WS.B.

QUART
Maison Vigneronne
Frères Grosjean* Fraz.
Ollignan 1. Tel: 0165
765283. (Vincenzo
Grosjean). F.TP.WS.B.

VILLENEUVE
Az Vit Renato Anselmet
& Figli* Fraz. La Crête.
Tel: 0165 95217 (Renato
Anselmet). F.TP.WS.B.

Since 1947 Valle d'Aosta has been an autonomous region within Italy with the same local government freedoms as the similarly mountainous border regions of Trentino and Alto Adige. Signs in Aosta are usually bilingual and the dialect of the local people is an almost impenetrable mixture of Italian and French that is more readily understood by the mountain dwellers on the French side of the border than by other Italians.

Valle d'Aosta is well known to skiers for its resorts at Courmayeur and Cervinia and to naturalists for the Gran Paradiso National Park. It is not well known for its wine even in Italy, but the whole area is now classified as a single DOC (see page 10).

Considering the fact that Valle d'Aosta is by far the smallest producer of wines in Italy with just 650 hectares of vineyards in all, and that those wines that have survived the pressures of modern economics count amongst some of Italy's most interesting rarities, the dedication of the whole area exclusively to quality production is justified in both wine and socio-economic terms.

After all, if the surviving vineyards fell into disuse, the physical appearance of the whole valley would change as the laboriously-maintained mountain terraces crumbled away.

The Aosta Valley
The Aosta Valley is famous for its chain of castles leading down to the Piedmontese border. There are 130 in all; some are now no more than ruined watchtowers, others were splendidly restored in the last century. The castles of Issogne and Fenis, both restored by the architect of Turin's incredible Borgo Medioevale, Alfredo d'Andrade, are most attractive; the fortress of Bard is forbidding. Fenis also has a museum of local history, the *Museo dell' Arredamento Valdostano*.

Some wines are made throughout the valley. Gamay is a light quaffable red made from the same grape as Beaujolais. Müller-Thurgau is made from the international grape of the same name. The same applies to Pinot Nero, but, unusually, it is also possible to find this as a white wine.

La Valdigne
The narrow valley of the Valdigne extends some 27km (17 miles) from Mont Blanc until just before Avise. The only vine that grows in this area, an indigenous one called Blanc de Morgex or Blanc di Valdigne, has the useful qualities of being able to survive at higher altitudes than other vines and of being resistant to the deadly disease phylloxera. The area produces a good white aperitif wine called Blanc de Morgex et de la Salle. The town of Morgex is the commercial centre, and La Salle has a notable castle.

La Valle Centrale
This area extends from Avise to St Vincent, where the road and the Dora Baltea river suddenly plunge southwards towards Piedmont. About 16km (10 miles) further on is the village of Arvier, with its intriguingly named Enfer d'Arvier, a light red wine with a pleasingly bitter aftertaste.

Still on the SS26 and a few miles after Aosta are the villages of Nus and Chambave, which give their names to two wines, which can be either red or white. Chambave in its white version is made from the Moscato grape. In its most prized form it can be made from partly dried grapes and have a formidable alcoholic content.

Torrette, the other particular DOC wine of the Valle Centrale, is a dry, slightly bitter red wine made principally from the Petit Rouge, another of the grapes indigenous to the Valle d'Aosta.

La Bassa Valle

The 25km (15 miles) of the Bassa Valle extend from St Vincent to the border with Piedmont. The vineyard terraces cloak the valley slopes.

It is when one nears the border with Piedmont that the land of classic Nebbiolo-based wines begins with the red wines called Arnad-Montjovet and Donnas.

These are made from the same grape as their heavier cousins Barolo and Barbaresco, but they are not aged for so long and can be much subtler wines. They are also very difficult to find outside their own areas of production.

The steeply-terraced vineyards of the Valle d'Aosta are clearly visible both from the fast autostrada and the winding superstrada. Viticulture here is laborious and expensive.

The Enoteche of Piedmont

ACQUI TERME
ER Aqui Terme Palazzo Robellini, Piazza A. Levi 7. Tel: 0144 770273. Fax: 0144 57627. Tue, Fri, Sat, Sun 1000-1200, 1500-1830, Thu 1500-1830. T.P.WS.

BARBARESCO
ER Barbaresco Via Torino 8/a. Tel: 0173 635251. 0930-1300, 1430-1800. Closed Wed, Jan, mid July. TP. WS.

BAROLO
ER Castello di Barolo Tel: 0173 56277. 1000-1230 1500-1830. Closed Thu, Jan. Museum. TP Sat, Sun only. E.F.G.WS.

CANALE D'ALBA
ER Vino del Roero Via Roma 57. Tel: 0173 978228. 1930-1200, 1600-1930. Closed Wed. Restaurant. TP.WS.

CANELLI
ER Corso Libertà Tourist information centre/*enoteca*. Tel: 0141 823431 *(municipio)*.

COSTIGLIOLE D'ASTI
Cantina dei Vini di Costigliole d'Asti Via Roma 9. Tel: 0141 961661. Fax: 0141 961471. Fri 1000-1200. Sat, Sun 1000-1200, 1500-1800 (1600-1900 in summer). Guided tours of castle. F.TP.WS.

GRINZANE CAVOUR
ER Castello di Grinzane Cavour Tel/Fax: 0173 262159. Closed Tue, Jan. Guided tours. Museum. Restaurant (Tel: 0173 262172). TP.WS.

The wine traveller in Piedmont is exceptionally fortunate; the system of public and private *enoteche* and *botteghe del vino* provides extensive opportunities for tasting and learning about wine.

The difference between the two types of wine showplace is one of size and scope. An *enoteca* will certainly display the wines of its area, but it will also often have a restaurant designed to serve complementary local foods and a museum of winemaking implements.

The *bottega* tends to be more modest, more specialized, often staffed by the growers themselves, and perhaps only open at the weekends.

There is a double pleasure in visiting the *enoteche* of Piedmont: they are all sited in monuments of historic interest that have been restored to serve as showcases for the local vinous heritage. Four of them are in castles, one is in a deconsecrated church, and two are in historic *palazzi*.

The castle of Barolo
It was, in fact, the annual Barolo tasting at the castle of Barolo that introduced me to the delights of Italian wine. My casual visit to a small village in the Langhe, whose wine I had certainly heard of but which I had never really explored, led me to the annual tasting of all 70 or so Barolos on display in the Enoteca for the sum of 5000 lire. The combination was enchanting – the highest quality Italian wine presented in a historic castle in one of the prettiest parts of Piedmont. I have been addicted ever since and still regard Barolo as the finest wine in the world.

Grinzane Cavour
If there is time to visit only one of these *enoteche* or *botteghe*, then that should be the Enoteca Regionale at Grinzane Cavour, near Alba. This is an imposing castle dating from the mid-13th century, which, as the name recalls, was once the property of the great statesman of the *Risorgimento*, Camillo Benso di Cavour. The prototype of the *enoteche* system, it was opened in 1971 as the showplace for the best wines and grappas of Piedmont.

Its wine selection is controlled by the splendidly named and, on ceremonial occasions, splendidly robed 'Master Tasters of the Order of the Knights of the Truffle and the Wines of Alba'. A restaurant within the castle serves Piedmontese specialities, and its museum has interesting historical displays on coopering, distilling, and truffle hunting.

The castle of Barolo is one of the nine Piedmontese enoteche. On display are over 100 different varieties of Barolo, Italy's 'King of Wines and Wine of Kings'. The castle also contains a hotel, school and museum.

LA MORRA
Cantina Comunale La Morra Via Carlo Alberto 2.
Tel/Fax: 0173 509204.
1000-1230, 1430-1800.
Closed Tue. Video show.
E.F.TP.WS.

MANGO
ER Castello di Mango
Tel/Fax: 0141 89141.
Closed Tue. On old Roman road *(Magistra Langarum)* from Piedmont to Liguria.
Restaurant. TP.WS.

NEIVE
Bottega dei Quattro Vini
Piazza Italia. Tel: 0173 671100. Wed-Fri 1400-1900, Sat, Sun 1030-1300, 1430-1900. F.G.TP.WS.

ROPPOLO
ER della Serra Castello di Roppolo Tel: 0161 98501. Thu-Sun 0930-1200, 1500-1900. Hotel in castle. TP.WS.

VIGNALE MONFERRATO
ER Palazzo Callori
Tel/Fax: 0142 933243. Mon, Wed, Thu, Fri 0900-1300,1400-1700, Sat 1000-1200, 1500-1830. Historic *palazzo, infernotto* cellars.
Restaurant. TP.WS.

Botteghe

There are many *botteghe del vino* in Piedmont, although most are only open at weekends. More are being established as small groups of wine-growers band together to take advantage of the growing public interest in genuine hand-made products of the countryside, of which wine is only one.

An increasing nostalgia for the countryside, combined with interest in *agriturismo* – holidaying in the country rather than in the traditional skiing or beach resorts – has created greater willingness on the part of the wine-makers to exhibit their wines.

Perhaps the most interesting of the *botteghe* is the Cantina Comunale of La Morra, near Alba. This is in the heartland of Barolo production, where every south-facing hill has its carefully-manicured Nebbiolo vineyard. You can find details of local vineyard walks here. La Morra itself is unique in having a statue not to a wine-maker but to *Il Vignaiolo*, the vine-grower.

Turin and its Vicinity

The Royal Hunting Lodge at Stupinigi on the outskirts of Turin. Those who think of the city as mainly industrial are amazed by the range of its architectural masterpieces.

COCCONATO D'ASTI
Az Vit Bava* Strada Monferrato 2. Tel: 0141 907083. Fax: 0141 907085. (Paolo Bava). 0830-1230, 1400-1900. E.F.TP.WS.B.

Piedmont may be more famous for its successful industries, FIAT and Olivetti; but for the wine lover it signifies the great Italian wines of Barolo and Barbaresco and exciting new styles of Barbera and Dolcetto. In fact Piedmont is particularly rich in wine; it boasts more than 40 DOC and DOCGs and the whole area is the first major wine producing zone in Italy to create its own umbrella DOC appellation system.

Turin and its vicinity
The city of FIAT, Juventus and La Stampa is often disparaged by Italians from outside Piedmont, and its ringroad system is successful enough for it to be bypassed as a matter of course by the car-borne traveller. But it has many attractions. This is the lovely arcaded city where Michael Caine was filmed in *The Italian Job*. It should be visited for its museums, palaces and churches, often built in a wonderfully extravagant

Torinese Baroque style. It also has some of the finest Liberty style buildings in Europe, dating from around the turn of the century, and an Egyptology Museum second only to Cairo's.

Terra dei Santi

Leaving Turin to the south-east by the SS10 to Chieri, you can make a brief stop at Superga, an extraordinary 18th-century basilica that looks out over the city and houses the Savoia Mausoleum.

Chieri is rich in 15th-century churches (S. Domenico, S. Giorgio, the Duomo), and is a centre for the production of a traditional Piedmontese wine that is rarely seen abroad, Freisa. The name comes from its strawberry-like bouquet and in both its sweet and dry versions it can be a sparkling red wine, not unlike a good Lambrusco, equally it can be made as a still wine with moderate ageing power, like Dolcetto.

After Chieri a diversion to Pessione leads to the fascinating Martini & Rossi winery and museum. The most impressive exhibits are the carts used to transport barrels for the new vintage's wine, all marvellously carved with appropriate scenes of Bacchic revelry.

The whole area is sometimes called the *Terra dei Santi* because of its associations with Turin's famous philanthropic priest Don Bosco, and the missionary S. Giuseppe Cafasso.

Fruit, wine and music

Malvasia di Castelnuovo Don Bosco is a sweet sparkling red that makes an excellent summer aperitif or, even better, livens up a fruit salad with a festive splash of aromatic wine.

I have to thank Roberto Bava, wine producer at Cocconato d'Asti, for introducing me to this combination of fruit and wine with his own Malvasia. Roberto's favourite theory is that the tastes of different wines can be matched with the sounds of different musical instruments; Malvasia is light, festive and summery - a piccolo, maybe? Cocconato is well worth a visit anyway for its fine hilltop views, its two good restaurants, and the rest of the Bava symphony orchestra of wines.

MONCUCCO

Bottega del Vino di Moncucco and **Trattoria del Freisa** Via Masso 6. Tel: 0141 9874765. Mon, Thu, Fri 1500-2400; Sat, Sun 0900-2400. Closed Tue, Wed. Restaurant and wine shop. TP.WS.

PESSIONE DI CHIERI

Museo Martini di Storia dell'Enologia (Martini Museum of the History of Oenology). Tel: 011 94191. Fax: 011 9419324. Book one week ahead for free guided tour and tasting.

TURIN

CHOCOLATE: SHOPS AND CAFÉS

Al Vej Bicerin Via Carlo Alberto 27. The complete *bicerin* experience.
Baratti & Milano Piazza Castello 29. Torinese gilt, mirrors and mahogany.
Pfatisch Via Sacchi 42. Turn-of-the-century time capsule with own chocolate workshop below the bar/ *pasticceria*.
Stratta Piazza San Carlo 191. Exquisitely packaged *gianduiotti* chocolates.
Zucca Via Roma 294. Turin's main street was re-built in Fascist style; this bar makes its own unmissable *gianduiotti*.

Chocolate and *I bicerin d'Turin*

Turin is also one of the world capitals of chocolate. Dynastic links between the royal families in Turin and in Vienna, together with a common cultural flowering in the early 19th century, meant that Vienna developed its coffee houses and chocolate cake at the same time as Turin developed the *bicerin* (pronounced 'bik-yer-in', and meaning 'little cup' in Torinese dialect).

The *bicerin* consists of hot chocolate, a small jug of hot coffee (both originally very expensive), and a small jug of hot milk. All three elements are left in their jugs so that the customer can mix them to taste in a large cup. Anyone ordering the *bicerin* in a café had the right to share a table with anyone else taking part in the same ritual. A whole ceremony developed around the *bicerin* in the coffee houses of Turin, and a special selection of 14 sweet biscuits evolved (called *I Bagnati*, literally 'the bathed ones'), each with its own name, to accompany the substantial drink.

Discover the typical hand-made Torinese chocolates, *gianduiotti*, in one of the marvellous mahogany, mirrors and gilt chocolate shops of Turin: the *bicerin* can be experienced, with all its ceremony, in several coffee houses.

Asti

Moscato vines in the Asti heartland of the Belbo valley.

Asti wines

Asti's great rival is Alba. While Asti has its historic Palio celebrations involving horse-racing every year, Alba has an almost parodic *Palio degli Asini* – donkey-racing. But in wine terms, the advantage seems to belong to Alba; how could Asti Spumante (now called simply Asti) match the splendours of Barolo?

The answer is, it can't; but if the occasion is right, it is actually much more appropriate. Asti is fun, Barolo is serious; Asti is light and low in alcohol. Asti is the drink Italians celebrate with – together with a good *panettone* cake – chilled, of course, and served in a flute glass to preserve the bubbles and concentrate the enormous floral bouquet.

Asti is not the only wine of the region, either. The two other principal wines are Dolcetto d'Asti and Barbera d'Asti. Here again, there is the comparison with Alba. True to type, Dolcetto d'Alba and Barbera d'Alba are more serious than their Asti counterparts; the Alba producers are probably making Barolo too, and there is often something of the 'junior Barolo' feel about them. The Asti versions are more nervy, brighter, sharper, more fun even.

It is Barbera d'Asti that is creating the news at the moment in the region. Producers have discovered its affinity with new oak. In fact, the naturally high acidity of the grape marries well with the vanilla cloak conferred by ageing in new oak *barriques* and the consequence is that Barbera has been transformed in the space of a decade from a wine that was unwanted to the smartest bottle in the restaurant.

South of Asti

The town of Asti itself is bigger and more commercial than Alba, as befits its status. It has a cathedral that is the supreme example of Piedmontese Gothic architecture, an impressive art gallery and a museum of the *Risorgimento*.

From Asti go south-west to Costigliole d'Asti, with its wonderful castle. It used to belong to the Contessa di Castiglione, who became mistress to Napoleon III of France, and is visitable by arrangement with the Cantina dei Vini di Costigliole d'Asti, the Enoteca belonging to the local producers' association (see page 18 for details).

From Costigliole go to Castagnole Lanze to browse in the Bottega del Vino shop, and then to Mango, to see the splendid castle and Enoteca Regionale (see page 19 for details). In medieval times it was the vital centre of the area strategically commanding the ancient Roman *Magistra Langarum* road linking Piedmont with Liguria. It now contains a restaurant and an Enoteca dedicated to Moscato wines and Piedmontese sparkling wines in general.

Follow the Belbo valley north-east to Santo Stefano and visit the birthplace of Cesare Pavese (1908-1950), the author who made the valley famous.

The next stop is Canelli, the commercial centre for Asti and a pretty hillside town, very conscious of its place in wine history. Further up the valley, Nizza Monferrato has an active Bottega del Vino (open Fri-Sun) and the Bersano Museum with its collection of prints and wine artefacts dating from the 17th century.

Return to Asti, maybe via Rocchetta Tanaro (see page 35), where the Bologna family make a range of pioneering Barbera wines, including the famous *barrique*-aged Bricco dell'Uccellone. The local foods to discover here include *Lingue di Suocera* (mother-in-law's tongues) bread (thin, crisp and flavoursome!), and the *Tirà*, a ring-shaped cake.

Loazzolo

Loazzolo, in the hills above the Belbo valley, is one of Italy's newest, smallest and most fashionable DOC areas. Inspired by the enologist Giancarlo Scaglione, a small band of producers have revived a long-abandoned wine type. This is Moscato Passito, a rich dessert wine made from partially dried grapes picked from sparsely-planted vineyards and small outcrops of vines dangling over steep drops, which are very picturesque, and very difficult to cultivate. As interesting as the wines in this mountainous area are the traditional cheeses of Loazzolo and nearby Roccaverano.

The village of San Giorgio Scarampi has a Bottega del Vino (open every day except Monday).

Castello Gancia in Canelli. Gancia were the pioneers of sparkling Asti in the last century.

NIZZA MONFERRATO
Bersano Piazza Dante 21. Tel: 0141 721273. Fax: 0141 701706. (Carla Cavallo). 0900-1200, 1400-1600. Museum. E.TF.WS.B.
Guasti Clemente e Figli* Corso IV Novembre 80. Tel: 0141 721350. Fax: 0141 727000. (A. Guasti). Mon-Fri 0830-1200, 1400-1830, Sat 0830-1200. E.F.TF.WS.B.
Antica Casa Scarpa Via Montegrappa 6. Tel: 0141 721331. Fax: 0141 702872. (Mario Castino). 0830-1230, 1400-1800. E.F.TF.WS.B.

MOASCA
Az Agr Vit Pietro Barbero Via San Giuseppe 19. Tel/Fax: 0141 856484. (Massimo Pastura Barbero). 0900-1830. E.F.TP.WS.b.
For further addresses see page 35.

Monferrato

FRASSINELLO
Az Agr Castello di Lignano* Tel: 0142 334511. Fax: 0142 563610. 0900-1200, 1500-1900. E.F.TP.WS.B.

OZZANO
Cantine Valpane*
Tel/Fax: 0142 486713. 0900-1900. Museum of wine-related implements. E.TF.WS.B.

SCURZOLENGO
Cantine Sant'Agata*
Reg. Mezzena 19. Tel/Fax: 0141 203186. 0900-1230, 1500-1900. E.F.TF.WS.B.

SERRALUNGA DI CREA
Tenuta La Tenaglia*
Via Santuario di Crea. Tel: 0142 940252. Fax: 0142 940546. 0900-1900. E.F.TF.WS.b.

TREVILLE
Pavese Livio* Regione Bettola. Tel: 0142 487215. Fax: 0142 487045. (0800-1200, 1400-1800. E.F.TF.WS.B.
Vicara (Visconti, Cassinis, Ravizza)
Cascina Crosietta. Tel/Fax: 0142 488054. Visit 18th-century church with *infernotto* and castle cellars of Castello di Salabue. Gastronomic weeks, cooking weeks and tastings. E.F.TF.WS.B.

VIGNALE MONFERRATO
Az Agr Accornero Ca' Cima. Tel: 0142 933317. Fax: 0142 933312. 0900-1800. Farm with 50 head of Piedmontese heifers. E.TF.WS.B.
Az Agr Nuova Cappelletta* Tel: 0142 933135. Fax: 0142 933550. Mon-Fri 0830-1230, 1400-1800. E.F.TF.WS.b.

The Basso Monferrato

From Asti go north to the Basso Monferrato. This area, between the Tanaro valley in the south and the Po valley in the north, is largely undiscovered and contains sleepy towns on the top of gentle hills covered with vineyards and woods. It cannot fail to charm.

Sometimes, indeed, it may even be a little kitsch. At the village of Callianetto, near Castell'Alfero, the villagers celebrate a character from the popular 18th-century *commedia dell' arte* theatre. This is Gianduja, a canny peasant who delights in poking fun at the pomposities of local worthies. The figure of Gianduja leads the local

Moscato grapes at harvest time in vineyards near Alba. Not all of them will go towards the making of sparkling Asti – the still Moscato d'Asti is increasingly popular as a dessert wine.

carnival procession of costumed girls from his native *ciobata* (cottage). Gianduja is now, of course, famous the world over because of the *gianduiotti* chocolates of Turin (see page 21).

Grignolino

The first wine town is Portacomaro, which has its own Bottega del Vino sited in the solitary tower that remains of the town's castle. It specializes in Grignolino and, a rarity indeed, Grappa di Grignolino.

Grignolino is a classic Piedmontese wine that is much undervalued – partly by the producers themselves, because of the difficult nature of the grape. It is almost a rosé wine in colour, but it has the structure of a full-bodied white wine. Needless to say, it is an excellent accompaniment to the rich local foods, especially the cheeses. But it is difficult to manage enologically, and poor versions of this wine are too common. As usual, the producer is the guarantee of quality, not the regulations that make this a DOC wine.

Nearby Castagnole is the home of a unique and rare red wine called Ruchè di Castagnole Monferrato, a dry aromatic red that is light in colour with a distinct hyacinth-like bouquet. Piedmont is full of such local curiosities that need a leading wine producer to take under their wing and promote as a re-discovery of an ancient heritage, which indeed they are.

Vignale Monferrato is only about 10 kilometres (6 miles) away and has the Enoteca Regionale (see page 19) in Palazzo Callori specializing in Barbera and Grignolino.

Frassinello

Frassinello, towards Casale, has two castles. The Castello di Lignano, a winery as well, is particularly striking with its round medieval tower faced with alternate bands of tufo rock and brick. Casorzo is another one of those Piedmontese localities with its own speciality wines; in this case Malvasia di Casorzo d'Asti, a pale pink wine that is usually sweet and either fully sparkling or lightly *frizzante*.

The Fair of the Fattened Ox

Moncalvo is the local market town and is famous for its food; *bollito*, delicious boiled meats, is a speciality. In fact, this is one of the few towns in Piedmont to retain its *Fiera del Bue Grasso* (Fair of the Fattened Ox), a festival day when a garlanded ox is the centre of a procession. Moncalvo was important enough in medieval times to have the right to mint its own coins. The ruins of the old castle can still be

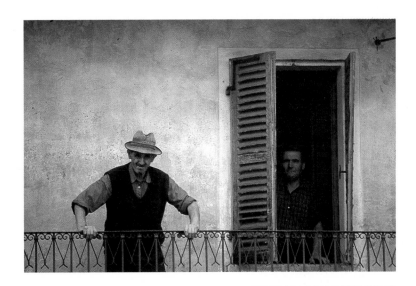

Most of the men and women who actually do the work of vine-tending throughout Italy belong to the older generation; what will happen when they have gone? Their children work in the towns. Their work is essential, and the question is increasingly pressing.

seen; the church of San Francesco, built in the Lombard Gothic style, contains notable paintings by Guglielmo Caccia.

North of Moncalvo there are wine producers to visit at the castle of Salabue and at Crea, the site of a remarkable Santuario, consisting of terracotta figures in a series of shrines, a sort of religious theme park from centuries past.

The infernal regions

Towards Casale, the commonest building stone is tufo. Blocks of this soft material form the walls of farm buildings, and conversely wine cellars are excavated from it, the famous *infernotti*. These secret wine cellars, also called *crutin* in local dialect, are difficult to visit because of continuous use, but the Enoteca at Vignale has its own *infernotti*, which can be visited to get an idea of these sanctuaries of wine.

BOTTEGHE DEL VINO
The following *botteghe del vino* (local wine promotion shops, see page 19) are open at weekends only:

ASTI
CISTERNA D'ASTI **Bottega del Vino** Tel: 0141 979126.
S STEFANO BELBO **Cesare Pavese Museum** and **Moscato Bottega** Tel: 0141 844918.

MONFERRATO
QUARANTI **Bottega del Vino** Tel: 0141 77081.
PORTACOMARO **Bottega del Grignolino** Tel: 0141 202666.

ROERO
CASTELLINALDO **Bottega Comunale** Tel: 0173 213069.

ALBA
DOGLIANI **Bottega del Dolcetto** Tel: 0173 70107.
NOVELLO **Bottega del Vino** Tel: 0173 731147.
SERRALUNGA D'ALBA **Bottega del Vino** Tel: 0173 613101.

Alba

ROERO
Cantina Ascheri Giacomo* Via G Piumati 23, 12042 Bra (CN) Tel: 0172 412394. Fax: 0172 432021. (Maria Cristina Ascheri). 0900-1200 1500-1700. E.F.S.TF.W.S.b.
Az Agr Angelo Negro & Figli* Fraz S Anna 1, 12040 Monteu Roero (CN). Tel: 0173 90252. Fax: 0173 90712. (Giovanni Negro). 0800-1200, 1400-1800. E.F.TF.W.S.B.

ALBA
Az Vit Ceretto Loc San Cassiano 34. Tel: 0173 282582. Fax: 0173 282383. (Bruno Ceretto, Bruna Manzone). Mon-Fri 0800-1100, 1400-1700. E.TF.B.
Pio Cesare Via Cesare Balbo 6. Tel: 0173 440386. Fax: 0173 363680. (Augusto Boffa). 0900-1200,1500-1800. Closed weekends. E.F.TP.B.
Prunotto Reg San Cassiano 4/G. Tel: 0173 280017. Fax: 0173 281167. (Danilo Drocco). 0800-1200, 1400-1800. E.TP.B.

Towards Alba

Alba is the capital of the Langhe, a wonderful area full of gently rolling hills with medieval castles and villages perched upon them. It is best visited in the autumn when truffles perfume the streets, the vines have turned russet colour and the new vintage froths in the vats.

In many ways Alba is the epitome of the Italian Experience. Churches built in warm red medieval brick, arcades, bars with gilt and glass, shops full of home-made cakes and biscuits, the aromas of mushrooms and truffles, and trattorias with ample menus. It is a marvellous centre for excursions into the winelands that surround it – the Roero and the Langhe.

Roero

North of the Tanaro river from Alba lies a hidden area of soft hills with soft and subtle wines. This is the land of two unique white wines: Arneis, fashionable with a distinctive almondy aftertaste; and Favorita, just

becoming known outside the area. The local red wine is made from Nebbiolo, the same grape that is used for Barolo, but here it makes a lighter style Roero DOC or Nebbiolo d'Alba with moderate ageing capability.

Visit the town of Bra for the finest Baroque churches in Piedmont and the unexpected delight of the Osteria Murivecchi, a wine bar/trattoria in the

courtyard of the Ascheri winery serving local foods with the Ascheri wines. Canale d'Alba in the north of the Roero region has the Enoteca Regionale for Roero wines (see page 18). It is also well known for its nougat.

Santa Vittoria d'Alba is the site of the enormous Cinzano factory and a town with a 'secret', according to the movie that tells the true story of how the inhabitants walled up the town's hillside cellars to hide their wine from the occupying Germans.

Barolo styles

From Alba turn south to the land of Barolo, a triangular area with its points at Alba, Cherasco and Dogliani.

Barolo, the wine, has a reputation for being something of a tannic monster, needing years to soften out. This reflects the inexpert application of old-fashioned vinification techniques when the wine would be fermented for as long as a month with the mass of grape skins continually submerged under the must, increasing the tannin levels all the time. The resulting wine needed at least five years in large Slavonian oak barrels to shed its mouth-puckering tannicity, even before bottling, and even then it rarely recovers.

Modern practice favours a much shorter fermentation with the necessary colour from the grape skins maximized by a process called *rimontaggio* (pumping the must back over the skins) while minimizing the harsh tannins that come from a more lengthy process. The wine is then put in barrel for the minimum two years, often with a short time spent in new oak *barriques* that give a characteristic vanilla-oak flavour, masking the tannins and adding a velvety touch to the wine.

Which style of wine is better? If handled expertly by a master winemaker like Aldo Conterno, the old style is incomparable, full of many layers of flavour and lasting for ever. Equally, a modern master, such as Bruno Ceretto, will produce wines that are a pleasure to drink from their very first year and gain in complexity as they age. Personally, I prefer my Barolo without new oak vanilla, but the style is very popular and very international.

Try Barolo for yourself at the Enoteca Regionale at Grinzane Cavour (see pages 18-19). This is an excellent place to learn about Piedmontese wines and truffles and, preferably, to consume both.

La Morra

Like Burgundy, the Barolo producing area is divided into sites that have long been recognized as producing

Vineyards encircle the wine town of Barbaresco, which lies north-east of Alba.

BAROLO
F.lli Serio & Battista Borgogno* Via Crosia 12, 12060 Barolo (CN). Tel: 0173 56107. Fax: 0173 56327. (Paola and Anna Borgogno). 0900-1800. E.F.T.F.WS.b.
Marchesi di Barolo* Via Roma 1. Tel: 0173 56101. Fax: 0173 56320. (Donata Patrito). Mon-Fri 0900-1700; Sat, Sun 0900-1200. Old bottles of Barolo from 1938. E.F.G.T.P.WS. (B for weekend).
Cantina Bartolo Mascarello* Via Roma 15. Tel: 0173 56125. (Bartolo Mascarello). 0900-1200, 1430-1830. F.G.T.F.WS.b.
Az Agr Luciano Sandrone Via Alba 57. Tel/Fax: 0173 56239. E.F.T.F.WS.B.

Serralunga d'Alba lies in the hills of the beautiful Langhe area and the heart of the DOCG Barolo zone.

CASTIGLIONE FALLETTO
Az Agr Vietti Piazza Vittorio Veneto 5, 12060 Castiglione Falletto (CN). Tel: 0173 62825. Fax: 0173 62925. 0930-1130, 1530-1730. E.TF.WS.B.

DOGLIANI
Az Agr Abbona Annamaria Fraz Moncucco 21, 12060 Farigliano (CN). Tel/Fax: 0173 797228. 0900-1200, 1400-1800. Wonderful views. F.G.TP.WS.B.

MONFORTE D'ALBA
Az Agr Costa di Bussia* Tenuta Arnolfo, Loc Bussia 26. Tel: 0173 77017. Fax: 0173 776305. 0800-1800. 18th-century cellars, museum. E.F. TF. WS.b.
Az Agr Riccardo Fenocchio Loc Pianpolvere Soprano Bussia 32. Tel: 0173 78335. Fax: 0173 78606. 0830-1200, 1430-1900. F.TF.WS.B.
Az Agr Elio Grasso Via Garibaldi 17. Tel/Fax: 0173 78491. (Elio Grasso). E.F.TF.WS.B.

superior wines. Vineyard names like Cerequio, Cannubi, or Brunate on a bottle indicate that the grapes came from one of these sites. *Bricco* is another common label word; it means 'top of the slope' and therefore indicates a site where the grapes will be of outstanding quality because of their long exposure to the sun on a hillside position.

La Morra is a small town in the middle of some of the best sites accounting for 40% of the total DOCG area. This is a town that is full of wine activities. The *Cantina Comunale* (see page 19) is an association of local growers where you can taste Nebbiolo, Dolcetto, Barbera, and, above all, Barolo.

One of their best schemes is the *Sentieri del Vino* footpath system for those who want to combine a healthy walk in the vineyards with wine tasting at a local producer's. Visit the Winery and Museo Ratti at the Abbazia dell'Annunziata nearby, which displays a wine artefact and documentation collection put together by the late Renato Ratti, the man who began the modern codification of the Barolo vineyards according to the quality of the sites.

Barolo
From La Morra retrace your route to the road to Barolo, and its Enoteca, housed in a castle with a hotel school and a small museum. It displays Barolo from over a hundred producers. From 1250 to 1864 it was the home of the Falletti, and it was the last Marchesa, Giulia, who is credited with the creation of Barolo in the 19th century.

The first reference to 'Barolo wine' comes, in fact, from the cargo list of an English merchant in the 18th century when war with France interrupted supplies from Bordeaux. But it was not until the Marchesa Falletti followed the French practice of vinifying the wine so that it would be drier and age longer that Barolo took on its modern form.

Barolo-producing territory is divided, roughly speaking, into two valleys, the valley of Barolo which includes the communes of Barolo, Annunziata and La Morra, and the valley of Serralunga, with the communes of Serralunga d'Alba, Castiglione Falletto and Monforte. Experts admire the Serralunga valley as the source of some of the biggest and most long-lived wines. Some say that Monforte is the top Barolo site of them all.

Dogliani
From Barolo take the road to Dogliani, whose Bottega del Vino is devoted to one of Piedmont's most attractive lighter red wines, Dolcetto.

The name derives from the sweetness only of the grapes, which used to be prescribed medically as the basis for a purgative diet. Dolcetto the wine is a smooth and very fragrantly aromatic dry red wine which has a slightly bitter aftertaste.

The return journey to Alba takes in typical picturesque villages of the Langhe. Stop at Serralunga d'Alba for its castle. The pink-striped winery down in the valley is Fontanafredda (closed to the public) which is sited at the old royal hunting lodge where Victor Emmanuel II, first King of all Italy, kept his mistress 'La Bella Rosin'.

Barbaresco

Barolo's lighter cousin, is how Barbaresco is described by those who do not know it. In fact, Barbaresco is often just as robust and often just as full-bodied, despite the fact that its obligatory ageing in barrel is one year less. As usual, individual styles of winemaking confound most generalizations.

But Barbaresco is much smaller in vineyard area than Barolo, and much more difficult to find outside its production zone. Angelo Gaja has made it famous, not least because his indisputably good wines are also some of Italy's most expensive.

By way of compensation, the wines of the local co-operative, Produttori del Barbaresco, are some of the best value and finest quality of any co-operative in Italy. One of the best places to taste Barbaresco is the Enoteca (see page 18), which is sited in the deconsecrated church of San Donato in the main square of Barbaresco itself.

The 'Four Wines' of Neive

Close to Barbaresco is the hilltop town of Neive, where high-quality Barbaresco is produced. Its ancient Town Hall is the site of the Bottega dei Quattro Vini, an Enoteca run by an association of 29 local producers.

The Four Wines have now grown into ten, reflecting the growth of popularity of new wine styles in Piedmont and the general development in sophistication of wine tourism and wine production.

To the original quartet of Barbera, Dolcetto, Moscato and Barbaresco, have been added Arneis (a local rediscovery), Freisa (ditto), Chardonnay (international style), Sauvignon (ditto), Nebbiolo (declassified Barbaresco), Passito wines (very fashionable), together with sales of grappa, mushrooms, truffles and hand-made confectionery.

LA MORRA
Elio Altare Fraz Annunziata, Cascina Nuova 51. Tel/Fax: 0173 50835. (Elio Altare). Closed harvest time. F.TF.B.
Az Agr Poderi Marcarini Piazza Martiri 2. Tel: 0173 50222. Fax: 0173 509355. (Manuel Marchetti). 0800-1200, 1400-1800. E.S.TF.WS.B.
Az Agr Ratti Fraz Annunziata 2, Tel: 0173 50185. Fax: 0173 509373. Mon-Fri 0800-1200, 1400-1700. Museum. E.F.TF.WS.b.
Az Agr Roberto Voerzio Loc Cerreto. Tel/Fax: 0173 509196. (Roberto Voerzio). 1130-1800. F.TF.WS.B.

NEIVE
Casa Vinicola Bruno Giacosa Via XX Settembre 52, 12057 Neive (CN). Tel: 0173 67027. Fax: 0173 677477. (Dante Scaglione). 0800-1200, 1400-1800. E.TP.WS.B.
Az Agr Giuseppe Mascarello Via Borgonuovo 108, 12060 Monchiero (CN). Offices in Castiglione Falletto. Tel: 0173 792126. Fax: 0173 792124. (Mauro Mascarello). F.TP.WS.B.

SERRALUNGA D'ALBA
Cappellano Via Alba 13, 12050. Tel/Fax: 0173 613103. 0800-1300, 1500-1900. E.TF.WS.b.

VERDUNO
Castello di Verduno* Via Umberto 19, 12060 Verduno (CN). Tel: 0172 470284. Fax: 0172 470298. (Gabriella Burlotto). 0900-1200, 1400-1900. Hotel. E.F.TP.WS.b.

CINZANO
The visit to Cinzano lasts about an hour and a half; it guides the visitor through the history and production of Cinzano sparkling wines and vermouth. The setting is the ex-hunting lodge of Carlo Alberto of Savoia. The visit begins in the sparkling wine cellars and proceeds to the vermouth plant where the hundred herbs and spices used for flavouring perfume the air.

The Cinzano Glass Collection in the villa comprises more than 140 rare glasses and the Historical Archives contain a fascinating collection of posters from the early part of the century.

CINZANO MUSEUM*
Strada Statale 63, 12069 S Vittoria d'Alba (CN). Tel: 0172 477111. Fax: 0172 479045. (Silvia Garattini). Mon-Thu all day, Fri-Sun a.m. only. Admission free. E.F.G.S.B.

Vercelli, Carema and Novara

The wines of Asti and Alba are so sumptuous that it is often forgotten that other parts of Piedmont are important for wine production, too.

The distinctive terraces with their stone *topioni* pillars signal the vineyards of the most northerly of Piedmont's Nebbiolo-based wines. Carema is a long-lived wine that has acquired something of a cult following among Italian wine lovers. The local co-operative that is responsible for almost the entire production also runs a Bottega del Vino exclusively to exhibit its Carema wines.

From Carema, continue south on the SS26 to Ivrea, the home town of Olivetti, which has a 14th-century castle and a good museum. A few miles before Ivrea at Borgofranco d'Ivrea look for the centuries-old *balmetti*, over 130 cellar-caves, still in use today.

Erbaluce di Caluso

South of Ivrea lies the town of Caluso and the zone of the curiously named white wine, Erbaluce di Caluso (loosely translated as 'green light of Caluso'). Erbaluce is a traditional Piedmontese grape that has been rediscovered and found to be very suitable for the techniques of modern vinification. Unusually, it can be used for Spumante, for still wines and for a highly prized *passito* wine (see Glossary) made from dried grapes. The ancient name for this wine is *vin greco* (Greek wine): wine was introduced to Italy by the Greeks, and *greco* is a term generally used in Italy for bunches of grapes that grow in two clusters rather than one.

Caluso is west of the Dora Baltea river which passes through Ivrea. If at Ivrea the traveller turns off the SS26 and goes east of the river on the SS228, the next important stop is the castle of Roppolo on the banks of Lake Viverone.

A medieval watchtower guards vineyards overlooking the town of Gattinara.

The Enoteca Regionale della Serra (see page 19) in this castle is probably better known to the tourists who come to holiday by the lake than to Italians. Its history, though, is intimately connected with wine – and is reflected in the emblems on the coat of arms of one of its first lords.

The story goes that one Carlo Beccaria, servant to Lothario I, alerted his master to a poisoned chalice that he was just about to drink. Thankful for his escape, Lothario ennobled his servant, and gave him the castle of Roppolo and the right to display his own coat of arms, which is still in evidence at the castle today: three chalices full of red wine on a silver ground. Carlo Beccaria then changed his name to Carlo Bicchiero (*bicchiere* meaning glass).

CAREMA
Cantina Produttori Nebbiolo di Carema Via Nazionale 28. Tel/Fax: 011 811160. (Clerin Muggiani). 0900-1200, 1430-1900. E.F.T.F.WS. (B for groups).

GATTINARA
Bottega del Vino Piazza Italia 6. Tel: 0163 864070. Thu, Fri 1600-1900; Sat, Sun 1000-1200, 1630-1930. T.P.WS.

Some of the historical associations of this castle are less pleasant, however: it is said to have the ghost of the knight Bernardo di Mazzei who was walled up alive in the castle in the 15th century.

The Enoteca specializes in the wines of the area around Vercelli and Novara: principally the Nebbiolo-based wines from around Gattinara, but Erbaluce from Caluso as well. It is also a hotel and restaurant, and outdoor concerts are held here in the summer.

Towards Milan

Taking the motorway E13 at Santhià and heading east, the traveller begins to encounter the rice fields that were originally planted to form a quickly floodable defence for Milan. Pasta as a food is a relatively recent addition to the northern Italian diet; risotto is more traditional here.

Exit on the SS299 at Agognate and the line of wine towns begins with Fara, then Sizzano, Ghemme and finally Gattinara. Lessona is a few miles to the east, Boca a few miles to the west. All of these towns give their names to Nebbiolo-based wines which have the potential to age well and are much lighter than their better-known southern Piedmontese cousins, Barolo and Barbaresco. The Nebbiolo in this area is called Spanna, and this is also the name used for wines that are not generally of the standard of those named after their towns of origin.

Of all these wines Gattinara seems to be the one with the most potential. History relates that viticulture began in the area with the Romans and that Cardinal Mercurino Arborio, the native of Gattinara who became Chancellor to Emperor Charles V, served Gattinara wine at court. Even 20th-century experts agreed that Gattinara was an exceptional wine –

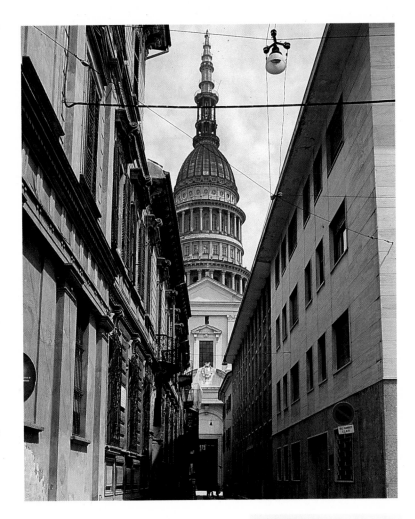

The spire of San Gaudenzio in Novara resembles Turin's more famous Mole Antonelliana.

until about 20 years ago, that is, when overproduction and bad cellar practices gave the wine a reputation as lean, unbalanced and tannic. Giving it the DOCG classification recently was the necessary impulse to change direction. Only about half a million bottles are produced every year by a very small band of growers. It is in their interest to upgrade the wine's image and quality. This is now being done: a visit to the Bottega del Vino in Gattinara itself is recommended.

GHEMME
Antichi Vigneti di Cantalupo* Via M Buonarroti 5. Tel: 0163 840041. Fax: 0163 841595. (Alberto or Giulio Arlunno). 0800-1200, 1400-1800. E.F.TF.WS.B.

MAGGIORA
Antonio Vallana e Figlio Via Mazzini 3. Tel: 0322 87116. Fax: 0322 87979. (Guy Fogarty or Giuseppina Vallana). 1430-1830. E.F.G.TP.WS. (B for groups).

Acqui, Ovada and Gavi

In the border lands where Lombardy, Emilia Romagna, Piedmont and Liguria intersect there are three distinct wine areas.

Acqui Terme and Ovada

A bare 18 km (11 miles) separates these two towns, one a spa in the plain, the other a border town in the hills. Both have a Dolcetto with their town names as a *denominazione*, though it is the Dolcetto d'Ovada that is attracting attention in the wine world at the moment. At last, in Ovada at least, this grape seems capable of producing rich, chocolatey wines with a good structure.

Acqui Terme, by contrast, is also well known for the sweet sparkling dessert wine that has become popular in North America, Brachetto d'Acqui.

Acqui Terme has been famous since Roman times for its therapeutic waters. Pliny the Elder was amused by the contradictory name for the local wines, *vinum aquense*, or 'water wines'. However, the town's coat of arms is an aqueduct with a bunch of grapes above it, and Acqui is still known both for its spring waters and its wine. Palazzo Robellini in the town is the site of the Enoteca Regionale, which specializes in the wines of this area. Acqui is worth visiting anyway for its cathedral, its castle and its museum of archaeology.

Gavi

Moving east from Ovada you come to the place of a wine legend – Gavi.

Gavi, the wine, shot to fame some 20 years ago as the local white wine, made from the Cortese grape. Called Gavi if it was within the larger *denominazione* area and Gavi di Gavi if it was in the smaller *classico* area, it was suddenly hailed by an influential journalist as Italy's answer to white Burgundy. It was, in any case, the most serious Piedmontese white wine that had appeared for a long time. Prices went sky high and restaurants began to demand a Gavi on their list at any cost.

Since then, the bubble has burst and Gavi is being re-evaluated. But, ironically enough, the wine itself has never been better than it is now. It may be comparable to a Mâcon – it has that steely fruitiness and moderate ageing ability. But Puligny-Montrachet, it isn't. It can take a dose of new oak, it can be made into a sparkling wine, but neither of these treatments are necessary. Enjoy it as it is, a superior white wine without being a Fine Wine.

Gavi the town is charming. It is dominated by an imposing castle and has a network of narrow windy streets at the foot of the castle hill.

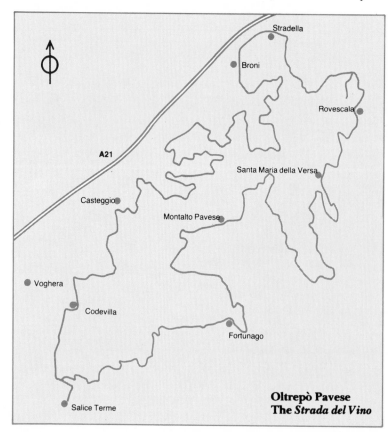

Oltrepò Pavese
The *Strada del Vino*

Oltrepò Pavese

These rolling, vine-clad hills are typical of Oltrepò Pavese – the land 'on the other side of the river Po.'

The *Milanesi* drink the wines of Oltrepò Pavese. Indeed, the villas and castles of this charming countryside of hilltop towns and villages are often owned by families from Lombardy's capital city.

As a consequence, the wines find a ready local market and are rarely seen outside the area. Don't be surprised to find that the young wines often have a slight sparkle to them, both the whites and the reds. This is quite deliberate; the food of Milan with the sticky delights of dishes such as *ossobuco* needs a wine with the freshness of youth and a refreshing sparkle to counteract its richness. Throw away all traditional Anglo-Saxon prejudices about what red wine should be like (old, full-bodied and complex, served at room temperature and made of Cabernet grapes) and you will find that what the local salami needs is a young, slightly sparkling, cool cellar-temperature easy-drinking wine, such as Barbera or Bonarda.

There is a well-developed *Strada del Vino* system to follow, and local producers are used to receiving visitors. Montelio at Codevilla organize day tours which take in visits to their vineyards and cellars, lunch in a local restaurant, a visit to historic monuments and the opportunity to buy local salami and almond cakes.

The Fugazza sisters at the castle of Luzzano are one of the region's best producers, and offer *agriturismo* opportunities and organized tours of the area with detailed itineraries. Each area has its own wine speciality. Rovescala is well known for its Bonarda. Santa Maria della Versa is famous for its sparkling wines, particularly from the highly regarded local co-operative winery. Canneto is the place of origin of two rare and colourfully-named wines, Sangue di Giuda (Judas' Blood) and Battafuoco (Sparks of Fire). Those who want an overview of Lombardy's wines should visit the Enoteca Lombarda at Certosa di Pavia, north of Pavia. The Certosa convent itself is a Renaissance masterpiece and should not be missed.

CASTEGGIO
Tenuta Peggazera* Via Vigorelli 151. Tel/Fax: 0383 804646. Mon-Fri 0800-1200, Sat 1400-1700, 0800-1200. E.F.TP.WS.B.

CERTOSA DI PAVIA
ER Certosa di Pavia Via del Monumento 5. Tel: 0382 925893. Easter-Sep. WS.

CODEVILLA
Az Agr Montelio* Via Domenico Mazza 1.Tel: 0383 373090. Fax: 0383 373083. 0830-1200, 1430-1800. E.TF.WS.B.

MONTÙ BECCARIA
Az Agr Vercesi del Castellazzo* Via Aureliano 36. Tel: 0385 60067. Fax: 0385 262098. 0930-1230, 1430-1830. E.F.TP.WS.B.

ROVESCALA
Az Agr Martilde* Fraz Croce 4a1. Tel/Fax: 0385 756280. E.TP.WS.B.
Castello di Luzzano* Az Agr M. & G. Fugazza. Tel: 0523 863277. Fax: 0523 865909. 0800-1200, 1400-1800. E.F.TF.WS.B.

S. MARIA DELLA VERSA
Fattoria Gambero Tel: 02 5454213/0385 79268. Fax: 02 5454576 F.TF.WS.B.

S. GIULIETTA
Le Buone Terre di Castello* Az Agr Marchesi Grimaldi, Casa Gian Pietro 3, Fraz Castello. Tel/Fax: 0383 899733. Fri, Sat, Sun 1000-1200, 1500-1800. Closed Jan, Feb. TF (TP for groups). F.WS.B.
Az Agr Isimbarda* Cascina Isimbarda. Tel/Fax: 0383 899256. 1000-1200, 1500-1830. E.F.TF.WS.b.

Liguria

CASTELNUOVO MAGRA
Az Agr Ottaviano Lambruschi Via Olmarello 28. Tel: 0187 674261. (Fabio Lambruschi). TF.WS.
Enoteca Regionale Liguria e della Lunigiana Palazzo Comunale. Tel: 0187 675166. Fax: 0187 670102. 0730-1330. Wide selection of Ligurian wines. ER.WS.

CHIAVARI
Enoteca Bisson Corso Gianelli 28r. Tel: 0185 314462.

IMPERIA
Enoteca Fratelli Lupi Via Monte 13, Loc Oneglia. Tel: 0183 21610.

MANAROLA
Cooperativa Agricoltura di Riomaggiore Manarola Corniglia Vernazza e Monterosso Loc Groppo. Tel: 0187 920435. Fax: 0187 920076. E.F.TF.WS.

The English Romantic poet Shelley set the example. English travellers have been attracted to the steeply sloping bay of the Italian Riviera for generations. Indeed, their old villas give the area a feeling of faded gentility even today.

Most wine produced in Liguria is for local consumption – and for the descendants of those pioneering travellers, who are now more likely to be making just a brief trip to Portofino. The peasant wine producer is a dying breed; working the steep slopes of the vineyards is difficult, and only a part-time activity for most of the vine-growers who remain.

Liguria's interest for the wine connoisseur lies in the tips at either end of its half-moon shape.

Soon after crossing the border from France near Ventimiglia, a left turn to the town of Dolceacqua brings one to the vineyards of Liguria's only serious red wine, the Rossese di Dolceacqua. Dolceacqua, with its ruined medieval castle and picturesque charm, is typical of the villages of the Valle di Nervia.

At the other tip of the crescent is the delightful area of the Cinque Terre. Only the first of these five villages, Monterosso al Mare, is readily accessible by car. But to reach the others it is a pleasure to walk the cliff path through the olive groves and the vineyards of Liguria's most famous white wine, Cinque Terre. This dry wine goes well with the local fish, but the most prized version is the dessert wine, Schiacchetrà.

Food of North-West Italy

Aosta

This is not an olive oil producing region, but the butter and cheeses are very good.
Cotoletta alla Valdostana: veal fried with ham topped with fontina cheese.
Carbonade: meat stew with onions and red wine.
Fonduta: Alpine fondue.

Liguria

Extra-virgin olive oil is the traditional all-purpose condiment, fish the traditional main course.
Pesto: ground mixture of basil, garlic, oil and pine nuts, a sauce for pasta, especially with trenette (pasta).
Torta Pasqualina: a savoury Easter dish made of puff pastry filled with ricotta and artichokes or spinach.
Fish: *baccalà* (salt cod), *bianchetti* (whitebait), *triglie* (red mullet).
Farinata: type of pizza bread made with olive oil and chickpeas.

Piedmont

The produce of the *contadino* (peasant farmer), such as maize, hazelnuts, apples, rabbits, pigs and oxen inspires the traditional dishes. In the rice-growing area of Novara soups and risottos are traditional.
Bagna cauda: fresh vegetables accompanied by a dip made with olive oil, anchovies and much garlic.
Vitello tonnato: cold roast veal with a creamy tuna fish sauce.
Brasato al Barolo: beef braised in Barolo.
Finanziera: lights and brains in a wine and cream sauce.
Fritto misto: mixed fried meats, brains and semolina.
Bollito misto: mixed boiled meats.
Bonet: chocolate pudding.
Carne cruda all'Albese: thinly sliced raw meat dressed with oil, lemon and thin slices of parmesan.
Gianduja: hazelnut chocolate.

A Piedmontese trifolau *or truffle hunter with his sharp-nosed hound – and a stick to make sure the dog isn't too successful.*

TRUFFLES

The famous white truffles of Piedmont have a season from August to January. Alba has its own truffle fair in October, but truffles are found in the hills of both Alba and Asti by the *trifolau* or truffle hunters, who use dogs to find their precious walnut-sized produce in pre-dawn excursions to secret locations.

Fortunes can be made by the lucky discoverer of good size truffles in good condition and it is only the smaller, less desirable ones that get as far as the shop windows of Alba.

The rest are sold privately for handfuls of cash that the taxman will have difficulty tracing. Dealing happens in brief early morning encounters as nuggets of truffle are produced from handkerchiefs in the arcades of Asti, Alba and Nizza Monferrato.

FOR FURTHER INFORMATION

Assessorato al Turismo (Piedmontese Tourist Board) Via Magenta 12, 10128 Torino Tel: 011 43211. Booklets include the excellent *Our Piedmont: short combinable itineraries for a long and unforgettable holiday* (suggestions from members of *Le Donne del Vino del Piemonte* – the Women of Wine in Piedmont).

Azienda Promozione Turistica Via G Mazzini 47, 19100 La Spezia. Tel: 0187 770312. Fax 0187 770908. Information on the Cinque Terre area in Liguria.

MAKING ASTI

Asti is not cheap champagne; it is a completely different type of wine made in a completely different way.

Champagne gains its bubbles by fermentation in the bottle – a laborious and therefore expensive process. Asti gets its sparkle from the Charmat transfer method, whereby the grape must undergoes slow fermentation at low temperatures in large sealed tanks. As carbon dioxide is given off in the process it is absorbed naturally into the wine, thus providing the sparkle, which is maintained by bottling carried out under pressure.

Continued from page 23

ROCCHETTA TANARO Braida* Via Roma 94. Tel: 0141 644113. Fax: 0141 644584. 0900-1200, 1500-1800. E.F.TF.WS.B.
Cantine dei Marchesi Incisa della Rocchetta* La Corte Chiusa, Via Roma 66. Tel: 0141 644647. Fax: 0141 644125. Sat-Mon, 1000-1200, 1500-1800. E.F.TF.WS.b.

North Central Italy

T hree distinct wine-producing areas make up north central Italy: the slopes and hills of the Adige and Isarca valleys which lead into Austria, the Valtellina that skirts the southern border with Switzerland, and the hills that are strung along the line between Bergamo and Lake Garda. Two regions of Italy are involved: Lombardy and Trentino-Alto Adige.

Lombardy is the industrial powerhouse of Italy, and alone is responsible for about 20 per cent of the gross national product. Milan is such a cosmopolitan city that it stands apart from the other widely differing principal cities of Bergamo, Brescia, Mantua and Pavia. Indeed, it is difficult to find a common characteristic for the Lombardi, a fact that is reflected in the wine production, too.

Many excellent wines come from the hills above Bergamo, from Franciacorta west of Brescia, from the Valtellina, and from the western banks of Lake Garda. If any wine is a leader at the moment, it is probably sparkling Franciacorta.

Trentino-Alto Adige is a very divided area. In 1918 what was part of the Austro-Hungarian Tyrol was given to Italy, and renamed Alto Adige. Later Mussolini tried his best to Italianize the region by settling industrial workers from the South in the area, and incidentally promoting the wine of Santa Maddalena to the official rank of third-best wine in Italy (the other two were more obvious and sensible choices: Barolo and Barbaresco).

The Alto Adige retained its independent spirit, however, and although German and Italian are the dual official languages of the area, German is more commonly used.

In Alto Adige about three-quarters of the wine produced is DOC, a high proportion for Italy, which in fact reflects the economic reality that it makes little sense in this area of mountainous labour-intensive wine production to centralize the wines to make a mass market product. This is also the reason

why the co-operatives of both Trentino and Alto Adige are amongst Italy's finest. With so much effort going into pendulous viticulture in steep vineyards, the wine had better be good.

Some of the best wines in Italy are now coming from the mountain slopes of the Adige valley, and the chorus of approval for Pinot Nero has been loud recently. But the Valtellina, that area of strong red wines lying to the south of Switzerland, seems stuck in a time warp. Like all the northern Nebbiolo-based wines, nothing much has happened to the likes of Grumello, Sassella, Inferno and Valgella. You may like them or you may hate them, but they remain resolutely old-fashioned in an exciting age of new grape varieties and ever-improving technology.

Franciacorta is another matter. Sparkling Franciacorta is now DOCG, and very proud of it, too. The leading producers, Ca' del Bosco and Bellavista particularly, have long made superb sparkling wines, and the Italians themselves can't get enough of it.

Franciacorta is also a naturally attractive area full of country villas, lakes and soft hills. It has also adopted wine tourism with enthusiasm; so a positive experience is guaranteed.

Silandro

SS38

R. Adige

Bórmio

Merano

Vipiteno

SS49

Brunico

Bressanone

Sassella

Sondrio

Grumello

R. Adda

Appiano

Caldaro

Bolzano

Ortisei

Ponte di Legno

Tresenda

Tirano

Édolo

R. Noce

Termeno

Cortina

R. Isarco

R. Sério

Mezzocorona

Mezzolombardo

SS48

R. Avisio

SS42

R. Sarca

San Michele all'Ádige

Cavalese

SS510

A22

Castel Toblino

L. Iseo

Cembra

mbaro

Arco

Trento

Pérgine Valsugana

Borgonato

Riva di Garda

L. Idro

Levico Terme

SS47

Rovereto

SS45B

L. di Caldonazzo

Brescia

L. Garda

SS12

SS236

San Martino
d. Battáglia

SS10

Mantua

R. Po

**PRINCIPAL
VINEYARD AREAS**

Valtellina

Alto Adige

Santa Maddalena

Teroldego Rotaliano

Trentino

Franciacorta

*Wine, cured ham and handicrafts are amongst many
local products for sale in the picturesque villages of
the South Tyrol.*

South Tyrol – *the* Weinstrasse

Caldaro is typical of the picturesque towns along the South Tyrol's Weinstrasse. Weinverkauf signs outside shops and wine producers' premises indicate that wine is for sale.

The wines

Most of the production is in the hands of co-operatives, necessarily so in this area where average vineyard holdings are so small in size. To their credit, it is the leading co-operatives just as much as the individual producers who are in the vanguard of wine development in this area.

Bolzano

Cornaiano

Appiano

Caldaro

R. Adige

N42

L. Caldaro

Termeno

A22

Cortaccia

Magrè

Cortina

**South Tyrol
The *Weinstrasse***

It is the bigger red wines of South Tyrol, varietals made from Pinot Noir and Cabernet, that are attracting the most attention in the wine world at the moment. Low yields from high-altitude vineyards and vinification using *barriques* are the characteristics of the new blockbuster red wines.

At the same time the whites are being made with good fruit and length, Chardonnay is gaining in popularity, and experiments with *barriques* help here, too. But the wines will never be cheap – the intensive labour involved in mountain viticulture ensures that.

CORTACCIA
Tiefenbrunner
Schlosskellerei Turmhof, Via Castello 4. Tel: 0471 880122. Fax: 0471 880433. (Christof Tiefenbrunner). 1000-2000. E.G.TP.WS.B.
Az Agr Georg Baron Widmann Via Im Feld 1. Tel: 0471 880092. Fax: 0471 880468. (Andreas Widmann). Closed Christmas - Easter. G.TF.WS.B.

MAGRÈ
Az Vit Alois Lageder Tel: 0471 809500. Fax: 0471 809550. (Alois Lageder). 0800-1200, 1400-1800. E.F.G.TP.WS.B.

NALLES
Castel Schwanburg Via Schwanburg 16. Tel: 0471 678622. Fax: 0471 678430. (Dieter Rudolph). 0800-1200, 1400-1800. F.G.TP.WS.B.

TERMENO
Cantina Vini Josef Hofstätter Piazza Municipio 5. Tel: 0471 860161. Fax: 0471 860789. TF.WS.

WINE MUSEUM
Südtiroler Weinmuseum Goldgasse 1, Caldaro. Tel: 0471 963168. Apr-Nov, Mon-Sat 0930-1200, 1400-1800. Sun, hols 1000-1200. Charge for entry.

Franciacorta

BERGAMO

GRUMELLO DEL MONTE
Carlozadra* Via Gandossi 13. Tel: 035 832066. Fax: 035 4420417. Closed Jan. E.G.TF.WS.B.

TORRE DE' ROVERI
Az Vit La Tordela* Via Torricella 1. Tel/Fax: 035 580172. 0800-1200, 1400-1800. E.F.G.TF.WS.B.

FRANCIACORTA

BORGONATO
F.lli Berlucchi* Via Broletto 2. Tel: 030 984451. Fax: 030 9828209. (0830-1230, 1330-1730. Historic cellars. E.F.WS.B.
Guido Berlucchi & C. Piazza Durante 4. Tel: 030 984381. Fax: 030 984293. E.F.TF.WS.B.

CAPRIOLO
Az Agr Ricci Curbastro* Via Adro 37, Villa Evelina. Tel/Fax: 030 7460558. 0830-1200, 1430-1900. Agricultural life museum. E.F.S.TF.WS. (B for groups).

The area between Bergamo and Lake Garda does not seem an obvious choice for the wine lover. The principal town of the area, Brescia, is better known for its steel mills and armaments factories than for its wines. But it is difficult to find a corner of Italy without sights to see and wine to discover; and this is no exception.

Bergamo
The principal DOC is Valcalepio, which comes from an area east of Bergamo, once the ancient domains of the Calepio family. The reds, made from Merlot and Cabernet Sauvignon, are more interesting than the whites, mostly Pinot Bianco and Pinot Grigio, although there are some good sparkling wines in the area.

Bergamo itself has a delightful medieval old town, the Città Alta. Don't miss the Colleoni Chapel at Santa Maria Maggiore and the Accademia Carrara museum of art.

Franciacorta
Once known as an area for rustic red wines, the Franciacorta area, just to the west of Brescia, has become famous as Italy's premier bottle-fermented sparkling wine area, while at the same time improving the quality of its still red and white wines. The first dry sparkling wine to gain its own DOCG appellation, Franciacorta is on the way to becoming a brand in its own right, synonymous with top-class sparkling wine.

No one is completely sure about the origin of the name Franciacorta. Some say it comes from the time when French troops settled in the area in the 16th century; others that it dates from the time when tax exemption was granted to the local monasteries. Whatever lies in its name, this is an area of gentle hills south of Lake Iseo full of villas that were built as the country mansions of the Brescian and Bergamasc nobility.

Franciacorta is just the other side of the Oglio river to Valcalepio. Start at Capriolo, a little hill-top town with medieval streets and some fine town houses. Its name derives from the roe deer which used to be common in the area. Go on to Paratico with its castle ruins and local legend that Dante composed part of the *Purgatorio* here.

Clusane, on Lake Iseo, declares itself *il paese della tinca al forno* ('the land of baked tench', fish from the lake, usually served with polenta).

Turning back from the lake towards the vineyards again, go towards Corte Franca. A neat inversion of Franciacorta, Corte Franca as a name only dates back to 1928, and reflects the common origin of the four villages of the new borough as rural domains, free from feudal dues after the drainage of the farmland by monks from San Pietro in Lamosa. (The monastery itself is at Provaglio d'Iseo – it suffered from neglect after disestablishment in 1817, but has now been restored).

Borgonato, the first village, has its history linked to the Lana family who constructed two *palazzi*, now owned by

ERBUSCO

Az Agr Bellavista Via Bellavista 5. Tel: 030 7760276. Fax: 030 7760386. Mon-Fri after 1000. Closed harvest time. E.F.G.TF.B.

Enoteca Le Cantine di Franciacorta Via Iseo 56. Tel: 030 7751116. Fax: 030 7751126. Wines at direct-from-the-cellar prices. WS.

Ca' del Bosco Via Case Sparse 20. Tel: 030 7760600. Fax: 030 7268425. 0900-1200, 1400-1800. E.F.TF.B.

Az Agr Cavalleri Via Provinciale 96. Tel: 030 7760217. Fax: 030 7267350. Mon-Fri 0900-1200, 1400-1800, Sat 0900-1200. E.TF.WS.B.

Az Agr Longhi De Carli Via Verdi 4. Tel: 030 7760280. Fax: 030 7709678. E.G.TP.WS.B.

GARDA

CASTREZZONE DI MUSCOLINE
Az Agr La Guarda* Via Zanardelli 50. Tel/Fax: 0365 372948. E.F.TP.WS. (B for groups).

LUGANA DI SIRMIONE
Az Agr Ca' dei Frati Via Frati 22. Tel/Fax: 030 919468. 0800-1200, 1400-1900. F.G.TF.WS.B.

PUEGNAGO
Az Agr Masserino* Via Masserino 2. Tel/Fax: 0365 651757. TF.WS. (B for groups).

RAFFA DI PUEGNAGO
Pasini Produttori* Via Videlle 2. Tel: 0365 651419. Fax: 030 2160300. 18th-century cellars. E.G.TF.WS.B.

For further addresses see page 45.

two branches of the Berlucchi family. Colombaro, nearby, has clearly visible origins as a fortified village.

Adro, a small town at the foot of Monte Alto, with many fine old *palazzi*, is the next stop. One kilometre (half a mile) outside the town, the church of Santa Maria in Favento is rich in votive frescoes.

The modern centre of sparkling Franciacorta wine is Erbusco. The church of Santa Maria Assunta has magnificent frescoes, and Villa Lechi, one of the many noble villas of the area, is unusually grand. Bellavista and Cà del Bosco, the two producers with the finest reputations for Franciacorta sparkling wines, are based in this area.

Castle enthusiasts might like to visit Passirano. Its well preserved medieval fortress was built as a defence against Hungarian invaders in the 10th century.

Borgonato, a medieval village with the two Berlucchi wine companies within its confines.

Lake Garda
The city of Brescia is surrounded by steep slopes, with the DOC wines Cellatica to the west and Botticino to the east. Neither denomination is of much more than local interest. The hinterland of Lake Garda on the Brescian shore, from Salò southwards to Sirmione, is not as well known as the opposite bank on the Veronese shore at Bardolino, at least in wine terms. But there are experts who say that the vineyards on the Brescian side are actually superior in quality.

Whatever the reality, the one wine from this part of Lake Garda to make an international impression is Lugana, a superior white wine made from the Trebbiano grape variety, here believed to be closer to Verdicchio in type.

Trentino

With so many tourists passing through from Austria on their way south and so many passing through from Italy on their way north Trentino is well organised for wine tourism (see page 45 for details of useful publications).

Trento, the scene of the Council of Trent (1545-63), is a good starting point for your tour. Visit the former palace of the Prince Bishops at the Castello del Buonconsiglio, and the Duomo.

Principal wines
Dry sparkling wines are a speciality of the Trentino wineries. The best of Italian *metodo classico* wines, Ferrari, is made here. Chardonnay is the up and coming white, but made in the fresh Italian fashion rather than aged in oak. Other whites to look out for are Pinot Bianco and Pinot Grigio, Riesling and Traminer. A curiosity is the Vino Santo, produced only in the Sarca valley from Nosiola grapes dried on racks and pressed about Eastertime.

Teroldego and Marzemino are the most famous Trentino reds. Caldaro, Lagrein and Casteller are lighter reds. The international trio of Cabernet Sauvignon, Cabernet Franc and Pinot Nero are increasingly popular; Trentino seems to bring out their aromatic qualities very successfully.

Cembra and Teroldego
From Trento go north to Lavis on the SS12 and stop at the Cantina Sociale di Lavis to visit their *Vinoteca* visitor centre for a tasting orientation of wines of the Trento hills and Cembra valley.

After Lavis turn east to Cembra for a pretty route up the valley, whose steep right bank is covered with terraces of vines. Cembra's co-operative, its Cantina Sociale, is the highest in Europe, and specializes in Caldaro and Müller-Thurgau.

Descending the valley again and taking the road to San Michele all'Adige via Faedo, the vines are trained in the centuries-old *pergola trentina* fashion that is unique to Trentino.

San Michele has the well-known Istituto Agrario Provinciale and Experimental Wine School in the buildings of an old monastery, where wines may be tasted. The folk museum here is also worth a visit.

BORGHETTO ALL'ADIGE
Az Agr Marchese Carlo Guerrieri Gonzaga* Tenuta S Leonardo. Tel/Fax: 0464 689004. (Luigino Tinelli). 0800-1200, 1330-1730. Museum. E.F.TF.WS.B.

CIVEZZANO
Az Agr Maso Cantanghel* Via Madonnina 33. Tel/Fax: 0461 859050 (Piero Zabini). 1000-1800. Historic cellars. Restaurant. E.F.G.TF.WS.B.

LAVIS
Casata Monfort* Via Garibaldi 11. Tel: 0461 241484. Fax: 0461 241043. (Lorenzo Simoni). 0800-1200, 1400-1800. G.TP.WS.B.
Cantina Sociale Lavis* Sorni, Salorno, Via Carmine 7. Tel: 0461 246325. Fax: 0461 240718. (Rosario Pilati). 0900-1200, 1500-1900. Visitor centre. E.G.TF.WS.B.

MARANO D'ISERA
Az Agr de Tarczal* Via G B.Mori 4. Tel: 0464 409134. Fax: 0464 409086. (Ruggero de Tarczal). 0800-1200, 1400-1800. E.F.G.TP.WS.B.

MARTIGNANO
Az Agr Maso Martis* Via dell'Albera 52. Tel/Fax: 0461 821057. (Antonio Stelzer). 0800-1200, 1400-1900. G.TF (TP for groups). WS.B.

MEZZOCORONA
Az Agr dei Conti Martini* Via Conte Carlo Martini 17. Tel: 0461 603932. Fax: 0461 603037. 0800-1200, 1400-1730. E.F.GTF.WS.B.

NOGAREDO
Az Agr Letrari* Palazzo Lodron. Tel: 0464 411093. Fax: 0464 414147. 0800-1230, 1330-1900. 16th century cellars. E.G.TF.WS.b.

Crossing to the other bank of the Adige brings one to the plains of Mezzocorona and Mezzolombardo. These are the towns of an excellent red suitable for ageing, the Principe di Trentino, Teroldego. Return to Trento via the hills and light red wines of Sorni.

Casteller and Marzemino

Wherever you go in Trentino, fortresses and vineyards line the route. There is a 'Wine and Castles' route in the Rovereto area and Rovereto castle itself has an impressive First World War Museum.

Marzemino, the red wine celebrated in Mozart's opera *Don Giovanni*, comes from Isera and the valley of Vallagarina. Further south, Avio is well known for the quality of its Casteller wine, a light red made from Lambrusco, Merlot and Schiava, taking its name from the Casteller hill just to the south of Trento at Mattarello.

A steep mountain road west from Trento leads to the attractive Sarca Valley also known as the Valley of the Lakes. Castel Toblino is a romantic lakeside castle surrounded by vineyards, and further down the valley in Arco there is an ancient palazzo. Tourist wine stalls, *punti di vendita*, increase in frequency nearer to Lake Garda.

Vineyards in the hills of Trentino blaze gold in autumn.

ROVERETO
Az Agr Conti Bossi Fedrigotti* Via Unione 43. Tel: 0464 439250. Fax: 0464 43963. (Rosanna Grigoletto). 0800-1200, 1400-1800. E.G.TP.WS.B.

Az Agr Longariva* Via R Zandonai 6. Tel/Fax: 0464 437200. (Marco or Rosanna Manica). Mon-Sat 0900-1200, 1500-1900. Closed Sun. E.F.G.TF.WS.b.

S MICHELE ALL' ADIGE
Istituto Agrario San Michele all'Adige* Via E. Mach 1. Tel: 0461 615111. Fax: 0461 650872. Museum.

Valtellina

The 'powerful wines and terrible
mountains' of the Valtellina were
noted by Leonardo da Vinci in his
travels. Both are much in evidence
today. The dominant grape here is the
same as for Barolo, the Nebbiolo (here
called Chiavennasca), but it produces
equally alcoholic, lighter-bodied wines,
best in the Superiore version which is
aged for at least two years, or the
Riserva aged for four. An excellent
heavier red is the Sfursat, a raisiny
passito wine made like Amarone from
partially dried grapes.

The wine route from Como

From the northern tip of Lake Como
the main road to Sondrio (SS38)
crosses the Adda after Morbengo, and
the regular pattern of stone-terraced
vineyards soon becomes apparent.
There are vineyards on both sides of
the Adda up to a height of 1200
metres (4000 ft) but the best are those
on the northern bank of the river –
they get more sun. The mountains
shelter both banks from violent
extremes of temperature.

Valtellina's sub-regions

Just before Sondrio is the first of the
four Valtellina Superiore sub-regions,
Sassella. Visit the 15th-century church
of Madonna della Sassella surrounded
by vineyards. The wine, like all
Valtellina Superiore wines, is best after
three to five years' ageing, and goes
well with roasts and strong cheeses.

After the provincial capital, Sondrio,
is the sub-region of Grumello, named
after the medieval castle, whose wine is
said to have a slight almond taste from
the traditional secondary blending
grape, the Brugnola.

Next along the main road is the
sub-region of Inferno, so called
because the hill terraces become so hot
in the summer. The wine is very long-
lived and takes longer to become ready
for drinking than its lighter cousins.

Tresenda marks the limit of the sub-
region of Valgella wine, almost all of
which is exported to Switzerland, the
traditional market for Valtellina wines in
general. Of all the Valtellina wines,
Sassella is said to be the best-structured
and the most refined; but, as usual,
much depends on vintage and producer.

*The town of Bórmio in the Valtellina. Well known
as a skiing resort, it is also the home of a herbal
digestif called Braulio. The onion-shaped dome of
the church indicates Austro-Hungarian influence.*

Food of North Central Italy

FOOD SPECIALITIES

Torggelen in the Alto Adige

Torggelen is a dialect word that came from the medieval word for the place where wine was served, and before that, from the Latin *torculum* meaning wine press.

Today, *torggelen* describes the very pleasant habit of late autumn trips into the countryside, where the colours of autumn trees and the last of the sun's warmth can be enjoyed at an outdoor table at the same time as the first of the new season's wine is ready. Roast chestnuts, homemade sausage with *sauerkraut* and *speck* (mountain-cured ham) are the normal accompaniments, served in the characteristic hillside *trattorie* or *weinstuben*.

Local cuisine

In the past Trentino and Alto Adige had similar cooking traditions based on shared Hapsburg and Slavonic influences. Now the Trentino has become more typically Italian regional, whereas Alto Adige has been at pains to preserve its own particular traditions. Trentino cooking does exist, but only in the home; it is not a restaurant culture.

Some dishes are common to the two regions. Soups are encountered more frequently than pasta, for example *canederli trentini* (*knodel tirolesi* in Alto Adige), a broth with *gnocchi* of liver.

Lombard dishes

Lombardy has given us some of the better-known Italian dishes: *Risotto alla milanese* – risotto with saffron; *Cotoletta milanese* – similar to *Wienerschnitzel*; *Ossobuco*; and *panettone* – the traditional Christmas cake.

Foods from Brescia

Naturally, the best food of Lakes Iseo and Garda is the fish from the lakes and the olive oil from the lakeside.

Rovato is noted for its meat. The plains of Brescia are a great source of cheese and butter. Some of the more noted cheeses are: Grana Padano, similar to parmesan, but not so expensive; Gorgonzola; and Taleggio, a semi-soft cheese from the town of the same name.

Specific dishes include: *Risotto alla pitocca* (chicken risotto); *Minestra mariconda* (pasta in broth); *Tinca all'Iseana* (tench roasted in oil, butter and laurel, coated with breadcrumbs, cheese, rosemary and parsley).

Valtellina meats and cheeses

The most famous product of the Valtellina is an international favourite: *bresaola*, cured and dried beef. There is a version made from cured goat's meat, *violino*, so called because of the traditional method of carving it in a way that recalls the playing of a violin.

In the province of Sondrio as a whole, specialities include: cheeses such as Bitto, Formaggelle and Stracchino; dishes based on mushrooms; and the inevitable corn dish, *polenta*, a staple of northern Italy, and particularly of Lombardy and the Veneto.

Grappa

Common to all the mountainous regions of northern Italy, grappa varies in quality considerably and can equally be nectar or fire-water. The producers of Trentino make a soft aromatic version of grappa using the gentle but laborious 'Tullio Zadra method'. This involves distilling in a *bain-marie* (gentler) and discontinuously (more control), to make refined grappas with elegant aromas. (See also pages 136-7.)

FOR FURTHER INFORMATION

Alto Adige Promozione Turismo Piazza Parrocchia 11, 39100 Bolzano. Tel: 0471 993808. Fax: 0471 993899. A wealth of information on wine touring in South Tyrol – hotels, itineraries and wineries.

Istituto Trentino del Vino Via del Suffragio 3, 38100 Trento. Tel: 0461 235858. Fax: 0461 239853. Map *Trentino DOC, Spumante, Grappa, Vino* and brochure *Itinerari Enoturistici* with wine routes and details of producers.

APT Rovereto Via Dante 63, 38068 Rovereto (TN). Tel: 0464 430363. Fax: 0464 435528. Booklet *Passeggiate tra Vini e Castelli* (Wines and Castles Visits).

Promozione Franciacorta Piazza G Bosco 1, 25040 Corte Franca (BS). Tel: 030 9826861. Fax: 030 9826954. *Franciacorta Itineraries* (also in English).

Continued from page 41

MOCASINA DI CAVALGESE Az Agr La Torre* Via Torre 3. Tel/Fax: 030 601034. (Attilio Pasini). 0900-1900. T.P.WS.B.

Continued from page 43

TRENTO Ca'Vit* Cantina Viticoltori, Via del Ponte 31, Loc Ravina. Tel: 0461 922055. Fax: 0461 912700. 0800-1200, 1300-1700. E.G.TF.WS.B. **Ferrari*** Via del Ponte di Ravina 15. Tel: 0461 972311. Fax: 0461 913008. (Massimo Sevignani). 0900-1200, 1500-1800. Closed weekends. E.G.TF.WS.B.

The Veneto

O nce the site of fierce fighting in the *Risorgimento* and World War I, the Veneto is a peaceful region, and its plains and foothills, decorated by villas and cypresses, are redolent of prosperity. Many towns proclaim peace on their statues of the Lion of Saint Mark: *Pax Tibi Marce Evangelista Meus.*

Set within the natural boundaries of the Dolomites in the north, the Venetian lagoon in the east, and Lake Garda in the west, it is easy to see why the Veneto has always been popular with the tourist. Its cities are rich in art and culture. Verona is famous for the opera festival held every year in its Roman amphitheatre, and for the Romanesque church of San Zeno with its marvellous medieval bronze doors; Vicenza is the city of the great Renaissance architect Palladio (1501-80); Padua has the basilica of Sant'Antonio, and Giotto's masterly fresco series in the Scrovegni Chapel; and Venice, of course, is unique.

While the Veneto does not produce anything like the volume of wine that comes from the southern regions of Italy, its wines are the most widely available of all Italian wines abroad.

Soave and Valpolicella, Bianco di Custoza and Prosecco, for example, are all instantly recognizable names, and the wines themselves are getting better and better as producers

The Lion of St Mark in Venice is both the symbol of the Evangelist and of the power of Venice's trading empire. Similar statues can still be found in towns throughout the old Venetian territories. The Latin motto translates as 'Peace be unto you Mark, My Evangelist.'

PRINCIPAL VINEYARD AREAS

- Prosecco di Conegliano
- Breganza
- Bardolino
- Bianco di Custoza
- Valpolicella
- Soave
- Colli Berici
- Colli Euganei

GULF OF VENICE

recognize the need for lower yields in the vineyards.

But, with the exception of the best Recioto and Amarone wines, few wines from the Veneto can be described as anything but 'everyday'. This is part of their charm, too. The traveller can easily grasp the very pleasant and unpretentious reality of wine drinking here, enjoying some of the most delightful quaffing wines anywhere in Italy. And, as always, there are still the individual producers to discover who prove the exception to the rule and make outstanding wines by any standards.

Verona and Soave

The medieval castle of Soave has a grand total of 24 towers.

GAMBELLARA
Az Agr La Biancara*
Contrà La Biancara 8.
Tel/Fax: 0444 444244.
(Angiolino Maule). TP.WS.B.
Casa Vinicola Zonin
Via Borgolecco 9. Tel: 0444
444608. Fax: 0444 444361.
Mon-Fri 0900-1200, 1400-
1700. E.F.G.TF.WS.B.

MONTEBELLO
Az Vin Dal Maso
Luigino* Via Selva 62. Tel:
0444 649104. Fax: 0444
440099. (Luigino Dal Maso).
E.TP.WS.

MONTEFORTE
Az Agr Prà* Via della
Fontana 31. Tel: 045
7612125. Fax: 045 7610326.
(Graziano Prà). 0900-1200,
1600-1900. F.TF.WS.
Az Agr Gini* Via Matteotti
42. Tel: 045 7611908. Fax:
045 6101610. (Sandro Gini).
E.TP.WS.B.

Verona is a charming city, particularly rich in Roman remains, Gothic churches and Renaissance palaces. Despite the almost uninterrupted occupation by tourists all year round, its people are invariably courteous.

Verona's importance stems from its location. At the foot of the Adige valley it has always been a natural meeting place for the Germanic peoples from the north and the Italians. Indeed, any foreigner in Verona is automatically assumed to be a *tedesco* (German) in much the same way as foreigners in Florence used automatically to be *inglesi*.

In wine terms, Verona can claim to be the centre of the Italian export trade through the specialist wine trade fair, Vinitaly, which takes place every April. Its most famous wines, Soave, Bardolino and Valpolicella, created the first wave of enthusiasm for Italian wines abroad in the 1960s and 1970s but subsequent overproduction damaged their reputation to such an extent that it is only now that they are regaining their respect in overseas markets.

Verona's local wines are not natural blockbusters in taste terms – they are the very opposite of New World brashness, which is one reason why it has been so difficult for them to regain international attention. But all of the wines have found ways to attract new interest. Soave has benefited from a realization that lower yields are essential for concentrating flavours, while the dessert version, Recioto di Soave, has found a place as one of Italy's greatest sweet wines.

It has been found that Valpolicella can be made much richer in taste if it is given a secondary fermentation on the lees of Amarone. Bianco di Custoza has a wide variety of permitted grape varieties in its formula. Therefore, increasing the percentage of an aromatic grape such as Sauvignon, for example, makes for a more interesting white wine. Non-traditional grapes, such as Cabernet Sauvignon or Chardonnay, are now also being fully exploited.

Verona's *Osterie*
Verona is rich in restaurants and *trattorie*, from the heights of the Michelin-starred Il Desco downwards. But a simple snack and local colour comes from the various *osterie* that can provide interesting wines by the glass in an atmosphere that is often more akin to a German *Weinstube* than a traditional Italian bar. The Bottega del Vino is the best – its Victorian Gothic Revival splendour is matched by a superb wine list.

Soave
The quickest way to Soave from Verona is by the motorway (Direction Venezia). Surprisingly, this route is also the most picturesque, the ordinary road out of Verona being one long piece of ribbon development.

The little town of Soave is instantly recognizable, with its picture-book medieval castle, town walls and gates, all remarkably well preserved thanks to enthusiastic restoration in the last century. The Enoteca in Via Roma and various gift shops attest to its concern for the tourist.

Soave as a wine has been much maligned. While there is no doubt that a great sea of indifferent wine is still produced under this name, new techniques of vinification, greater attention to work in the vineyards and the reduction of yields (grapes per hectare) have done much to revive the fortunes of this wine. The latest developments include official sanction for the addition of Chardonnay to the blend of grapes that make up the wine (principally Garganega, the most important, and Trebbiano). This move has led to protests about loss of native character and 'internationalization' of Soave's taste characteristics. As always, the producer is the key factor.

Smaller producers with serious wines, such as Pieropan and Anselmi, have always been admired. But it is significant that the mass market producers, who in the past have so often been criticized for their bland white wines, have now started to gain attention for new Soaves. These wines have more body and character and even benefit from three or four years' ageing.

Gambellara

One more motorway stop, or about 10 more kilometres (6 miles) towards Vicenza is the town of Gambellara, home of the Zonin company, Italy's largest private winemaking concern. The company has vineyards in all the major wine producing areas of Italy, but naturally, it also produces the white wine called Gambellara, which is very similar to Soave in its make-up. Zonin's most famous version of the wine is an unusual variation of style: *Recioto* (sweet and made from dried grapes) and *Spumante* (sparkling).

SOAVE
Az Agr Pieropan Via Camuzzoni 3. Tel: 045 6190171. Fax: 045 6190040. (Teresita Pieropan). Mon-Fri 0900-1200, 1400-1800. F.TP.WS.B.

VERONA
F.lli Pasqua Via Belviglieri 30. Tel: 045 8402111. Fax: 045 8402121. (Carlo Pasqua). 0900-1230, 1500-1900. E.F.G.TF.WS.B.
Villa Mattarana (Az Agr Zamuner) Via Mattarana 32. Tel: 045 8342168. Fax: 045 8343750. (Gabriella Tomat, Alessandra Zamuner). Cantina in Custoza, but tastings at historic villa. *Agriturismo.* E.F.TP.WS.B.

WINE BAR
La Bottega del Vino Via Scudo di Francia 3, Verona. Tel: 045 8004535 Closed Tue.

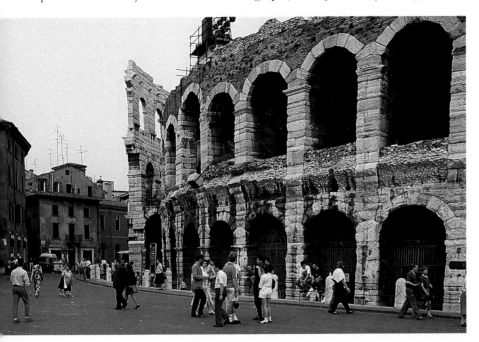

The Roman arena of Verona is part of the rich historic legacy of a city that is home to the wine fair Vinitaly. Verona is also the chief city of the region that produces Bardolino, Soave and Valpolicella.

Bardolino

Bardolino and a drive in the area with a stop for wine tasting makes for a pleasant excursion.

Verona to Lake Garda
From Verona take the main road to Lake Garda and the town of Peschiera del Garda, an important Austrian stronghold in the years before the great national uprising, the *Risorgimento*. There are remains of the 19th-century fort. To the south lies Bianco di Custoza land, to the north, after a small overlap with Bianco di Custoza, is the territory of Bardolino. The town of Lazise retains its characteristic crenellations, dating from the time when it was the Venetian Republic's main outlet on to Lake Garda. It has an Enoteca in Via Porta del Lion.

Bardolino
Bardolino itself is a small tourist-orientated town of some charm; but in season it is totally impossible to park nearby and the streets themselves are too narrow to admit traffic anyway. Do not miss the 11th-century frescoed church of San Severo just by the main road out of Bardolino to Garda.

All of the town's grocery shops and a couple of specialist wine shops sell Bardolino wine, especially that of the most prominent local producer, Azienda Agricola Guerrieri Rizzardi. Countess Rizzardi's villa takes up the southern flank wall of the town and a doorway in this wall leads to the villa's own small museum of winemaking implements, and its wineshop. All the Guerrieri Rizzardi wines are estate bottled and the Countess is a proponent of organic cultivation for the vineyards and non-pasteurization for the wines. She has introduced single vineyard versions of all her wines and the quality is consistently high.

BARDOLINO
Az Agr Guerrieri Rizzardi* Piazza Guerrieri 1. Tel: 045 7210028. Fax: 045 7210704. 0830-1200, 1530-1800. E.G.WS.B.
Az Agr F.illi Zeni* Via Costabella 9. Tel: 045 7210022. Fax: 045 6212702. Museum. E.G.TP.WS.B.

CAVAION VERONESE
Az Agr Le Fraghe* La Colombara, 37010 Cavaion Veronese. Tel: 045 7236832. Fax: 045 6260183. 0800-1200, 1400-1700. E.G.TF.WS.b.

Bardolino is a very ancient wine, but not a pretentious one; it is a light, fruity red with a characteristic cherry-stone taste. Normally a bright garnet colour, it is also made in the rosé Chiaretto version that is a perfect summer day's picnic wine.

The signposts for the Bardolino *Strada del Vino* will take you to producers who sell to the public, advertising the fact with their *punto di vendita* signs. Of course, the fact that there is a steady tourist traffic in the area means that the actual quality of the wine can be variable. In fact, the myth of the 'peasant who makes wonderful wine just like they used to in the old days' is largely just that. Nevertheless, there are some charming little towns in the soft hills above

The hills of Bardolino

From Bardolino the *Strada del Vino* leads the traveller to Affi, Cavaion, Calmasino, Pastrengo, Sandrà, Colà, Castelnuovo del Garda, and back to Peschiera. These small villages in the range of hills between Lake Garda and the Adige valley are the heartland of Bardolino and have numerous *punti di vendita* for both wine and olive oil.

An interesting diversion is from Affi to Rivoli Veronese, the site of a Napoleonic victory in 1797 and now a monument and museum. The castle just outside the village looks down the valley of the Adige, the invasion route from the north.

OLIVE OIL

The pale yellow extra-virgin olive oil of Lake Garda is, as might be expected, the most perfect olive oil for fish. Lighter and milder than Tuscan olive oil, and definitely not peppery at all, Lake Garda oil is soft and fruity.

The Olive Oil Route signposts indicate a trail along the shore of the Lake, the *Riviera degli Olivi*, intertwined with the *Strada del Vino*, and just before Cisano there is an olive oil museum. Locals swear that the oil is a particular delicacy and a paradigm of the organic because the microclimate of Lake Garda does not permit the survival of parasites on the olive fruit, which in other regions might have to be destroyed with chemical sprays. Visit the modern olive oil mill (*frantoio*) on the road out of Calmasino to Cavaion to buy the genuine extra-virgin local oil.

The wine town of Bardolino has a maze of narrow streets. The town is pleasantly placed on the shores of Lake Garda: its delicatessens are well stocked with local wines.

12% Alcohol by volume

750 ML e

TACCHETTO

Bardolino
denominazione di origine controllata
classico
imbottigliato all'origine dal viticoltore
GUERRIERI RIZZARDI · VERONA · ITALIA

Product of Italy   ESTATE BOTTLED   Dry red wine

DOLCE
Az Agr Armani Albino*
Loc Ceradello 401.
Tel/Fax: 045 7290023.
0800-1200, 1400-1700.
E.TF.WS.B.

OLIVE OIL PRODUCER
Frantoio Olive Calmasino Via Monte Baldo 14, Calmasino. Tel: 045 7235598. Mon-Sat 0900-1330, 1500-1900.

OLIVE OIL MUSEUM
Museo dell'Olio Oleificio Cisano del Garda, Calmasino. Mon-Sat 0830-1230, 1500-1900. Sun 0830-1230.

Custoza

Bianco di Custoza takes its name from the historic town of Custoza about 18km (11 miles) south-west of Verona. As a wine it is enjoying considerable success as an alternative to Soave, partly because it has none of Soave's image problems, but mostly because the permitted *uvaggio*, the blend of grapes, includes aromatic varieties, such as Sauvignon, which can be used to make more interesting wines.

At its best this is a light, fragrant and fruity white wine to be drunk within 18 months or so of production. As with the whole area around Lake Garda, viticulture has ancient traditions here, and probably early origins. Wine production here can be traced back to the 1st century AD.

Of all the wine roads near Verona, these are the most clearly marked, an unusual pleasure. It is easy to follow the main *Strada del Vino* with its *punto di vendita* signs, and there are several large roadside hoardings which advertise the route and its points of interest.

Custoza – the wine route
The starting point for the traveller from Verona is a turning off the motorway about 10km (6 miles) west of Verona, to the town of Sommacampagna. Here one picks up signs for the *Strada del Vino* and finds several *punti di vendita*.

Sommacampagna itself is a noted centre for wine production; records referring to the medieval town of Summacampania (it is more like a village today), prove that vineyards flourished here in AD 938.

Just outside Sommacampagna, on the way to Custoza, there is a large sign or hoarding showing the wine route, which may be useful for planning the rest of the trip.

Custoza – the town
Custoza is a small town situated on two hills, each dominated by a particular building. On the highest hill is the Ossario di Custoza, a monument and an ossuary.

The Ossario di Custoza

This ossuary (literally a bone house, or burial vault) contains the remains of the Austrian and Piedmontese dead of the two battles at Custoza during the *Risorgimento*.

The monument is an imposing needle-shaped structure built at the end of the 19th century. It is open to the public and, on a fine day, is a wonderful vantage point, with views over the immense plain of the Mincio river and hills around the south of Lake Garda.

You can see the hillsides of Bianco di Custoza production lying in a semicircle to the north of the town.

The other hill of Custoza is topped by the Villa Pignatti Morano, a grand building restored in the 1930s but retaining in its walls the pockmarks of 19th-century battles. Once past the hilltop villa, the *Strada del Vino* forks, left to Villafranca, right to Valéggio sul Mincio. On the way down the hill to Villafranca there is a *punto di vendita* with demijohns of wine displayed outside. This is an attractively wooded area with winding country roads.

Valéggio is dominated by a hilltop medieval castle and has a botanical park in the grounds of the Villa Segurtà. From Valéggio the *Strada del Vino* goes to Peschiera del Garda, where the Bianco di Custoza zone overlaps with Bardolino.

Villa Pignatti Morano is the first sight of Custoza for the traveller approaching from Villafranca.

CORTE GARDONI

1991

Bianco di Corte

BIANCO DI CUSTOZA
Denominazione di Origine Controllata

Messo in bottiglia all'origine da
Azienda Agricola Corte Gardoni di Gianni Piccoli
Valeggio sul Mincio - Italia

750 ml ℮ 12% vol.

®

Valpolicella

The Masi winery, one of the top producers of Valpolicella, is set in gently rolling countryside, surrounded by vineyards and cherry trees.

Valpolicella is produced on the north bank of the Adige in the foothills of the Lessini mountains. The area to the west of Verona from Pedemonte to Sant'Ambrògio is the Classico area, but the Valpolicella of the Pantena valley can confound expectations and age very well.

Valpolicella

Valpolicella can be a delight, full of fragrance and flavour. At its best it is a bright, fruity, medium-weight red wine, with a dry finish and a pleasantly bitter cherry-stone aftertaste. At its worst the chemical treatments needed to rectify poor-quality wine overwhelm it with a sulphurous prickle. Fortunately, it is more and more difficult to find really bad wines.

The secret of Valpolicella lies in its grapes, its vinification and its site. The role that each of its constituent grapes plays has been the subject of much research, but basically the two grapes that give weight to the wine are Corvina (now successfully vinified by some growers as a mono-varietal) and Rondinella. Molinara adds a certain spiciness and the other two, Negrara and Rossignola, are traditional, but added in tiny quantities.

The wine has always been made for drinking two or three years after the vintage. Recently, however, some producers have been making longer-lived versions. Masi's Campo Fiorin for example, is made by re-fermenting the wine in what is called the *ripasso* ('passed over again') method on the base of Amarone pressings (the rich pomace left after dried Amarone grapes have been finally crushed).

Producers are basically in agreement that the vanilla wood tastes of new oak overwhelm Valpolicella, but the fact that foreign markets love oak means that experiments continue in the reconciliation of the two tastes.

In general, the use of oak tends to obscure the bright cherry fruit tastes of Valpolicella.

Out of Verona

Romano Dal Forno is an up-and-coming winemaker based east of Verona who is attracting much praise from the wine critics for his Valpolicella and Amarone. However, he is the exception that proves the rule. Most of the well-known producers are to be found to the north-west of Verona between Pedemonte and Sant'Ambrògio.

You can make an interesting excursion, combining the pleasure of wine travelling with the sight of magnificent mountain scenery, by driving up the Valpantena from Verona and then descending into the Valpolicella.

From Verona take the road to Grezzana, due north of the city. The Cantina Sociale of Valpantena has signs of the Consorzio for Valpolicella indicating the zone of production. The bishop in their logo is San Zeno, patron saint of Verona.

Just before Grezzana on the left of the road is the imposing Palladian Villa Arvedi, often used for official wine presentations. This area is where Bertani's Valpolicella Valpantena, a long-lived version of this famous wine, is produced.

Valpolicella Classico

By following the winding road up past the marble quarries of the Valpantena, you will eventually emerge into mountain landscape. At Fosse the descent begins into the Progno valley and the Valpolicella whose territory is indicated by vineyards and cherry trees (which have the added function of binding the earth of the vineyard terraces with their roots).

From the attractive town of Fumane, take another winding road to Marano, up through the olive tree and vine plantations. There are several *punto di vendita* signs from now on, but *vino contadino* (home-made wine) can be a trap: it is rarely good quality unless, as does happen, the *contadino* has bought his wine from the local co-operative.

CELLORE D'ILLASI
Az Agr Romano Dal Forno Loc Lodoletta 4. Tel/Fax: 045 7834923. (Romano Dal Forno). 0800-1200, 1500-1900. TF.WS.B.

FUMANE
Allegrini Via Giare 7. Tel: 045 7701138. Fax: 045 7701774. 0900-1230, 1430-1830. TP (with snack). WS.B.

GARGAGNAGO
Masi Via Monteleone. Tel: 045 7703622. Fax: 045 7703523. (Monica Marogna). 0800-1200, 1400-1800. E.F.G.TP.WS.B.
Serègo Alighieri Via Stazione 2. Tel: 045 7703622. Fax: 045 7703523. (Monica Marogna). 0800-1200, 1400-1800. *Agriturismo*, wine shop. E.F.G.TP.WS.B.

NEGRAR
Guerrieri Rizzardi* Villa Rizzardi Poiega. Tel: 045 7210028. Fax: 045 7210704. (Sig.na Elena). 0830-1800. 18th-century garden. E.F.G.TP.WS.B.
Az Agr Roberto Mazzi e Figli* Fraz Sanperetto, Via Crosetta 8. Tel: 045 7502072. Fax: 045 8266150. 0900-1200, 1400-1830. E.G.TF.WS.b.

PEDEMONTE
Bolla* Via Alberto Bolla 3. Tel: 045 8670911. Fax: 045 8670912. (Simonetta Taccuso). Mon-Thu 0830-1300, 1400-1700, Fri 0830-1300. E.TF (first two wines). WS.B.
Santa Sofia* Via Ca' Dede' 61. Tel: 045 7701074. Fax: 045 7703222. (Patrizia or Luciano Begnoni). 0900-1200, 1430-1800. E.TP.WS.B.
Tedeschi* Via G. Verdi 4. Tel: 045 7701487. Fax: 045 7704239. (Antonietta Tedeschi). 0800-1200, 1400-1800. E.TF.WS.B.

S FLORIANO
Brigaldara* Tel: 045 7701065. Fax: 045 680034. (Stefano Cesari). E.F.TF.WS.B.

S PIETRO IN CARIANO
Tenuta Pule Az Agr S Pietro* Via Monga 9. Tel: 045 7701246. Fax: 045 6800275. (Roberto Marconi, Camilla Galtarossa). 1000-1900. E.G.TP.WS.B.

The gentle arc of hills near Fumane, the heart of the Valpolicella, where vines and cherry trees intermingle.

RECIOTO AND AMARONE
Recioto is a sweet red wine, not unlike a young Port. Amarone is a rich raisiny wine with an attractive bitter twist to the finish. These are the prestige wines of the Valpolicella. The start of the process is the same for both wines.

Selected grapes, mostly Corvina, are picked when fully ripe and laid out on wicker racks in drying lofts. The microclimate creates ideal conditions for the wind to dry these grapes naturally until their sugars are concentrated and they have sufficiently shrivelled in size to produce long-lived sipping wines (*vini da meditazione*, the Italians call them).

Complete fermentation of the sugar-rich must that is the eventual result of pressing the dried grapes leads to a raisiny wine with a dry finish, Amarone (literally 'the big bitter one'); while prematurely arrested fermentation leaves a sweet dessert wine, Recioto. Both wines are wonderful with cheese.

San Floriano and San Giorgio
At the end of the valley you come to San Floriano. The Romanesque church at the crossroads is one of the most important in the Veneto.

Here one can either turn left to Pedemonte, glimpsing the rustic Palladian Villa Serègo (not open to the public), now the headquarters of the Santa Sofia wine company, or right to Sant'Ambrògio, an important centre for Classico wines

Just above Sant'Ambrògio in the hills is the village of San Giorgio, with an important Romanesque church and a delightful *trattoria*. Don't miss the Serègo Alighieri estate, owned by direct descendants of Dante since the 14th century and now one of Valpolicella's leading producers.

Another agreeable excursion is to the Villa Rizzardi Poiega in Negrar, with its famous 18th-century gardens. It has a wine-tasting room in the courtyard.

Vicenza and Padua

The two towns of Padua and Vicenza are often passed over by the tourist in search of the more famous delights of Venice in the east and Verona to the west. Giotto's Cappella degli Scrovegni in Padua and Palladio's Teatro Olimpico in Vicenza are my personal favourite buildings in these two towns. The wine lover has then only to go into the hills to the south to find the old country estates of the urban nobility, as well as two modern wine routes.

Padua – the Colli Euganei

There are no fewer than 13 DOC wines in this area, ranging from the ubiquitous Cabernet and Chardonnay to the highly perfumed Moscato Fior d'Arancio. This is said to have been the cause of the great poet Petrarch's conversion to wine in 1370 when he arrived at the town subsequently called Arquà Petrarca in his honour.

Vicenza – the Colli Berici

The origins of viticulture in this area go back to at least 3000 BC. More recently, this area was the first to provide wines for the city of Venice in the times of the Republic. The countryside is dotted with numerous Palladian villas, including La Rotonda, the most famous of them all, Villa Pagafetta Camerini and Villa Valmarana ai Nani, just to name a few of the most important.

Colli Berici's most typical wine is the Tocai Rosso, a light and fruity red that, despite the name, has nothing to do with its more famous Hungarian namesake. It is light enough to accompany Vicenza's most famous gastronomic dish, *baccalà*, a stew of dried stockfish whose origins date back to Venetian trading with the Hanseatic League of the Baltic Sea.

Vicenza, city of the great Renaissance architect Palladio.

Breganze: the *Strada del Vino*

Just north of Vicenza, near some of the finest Venetian villas (don't miss the frescoed Castello di Thiene), is the ancient town of Breganze. This is the centre of a DOC wine zone with a signposted *Strada del Vino* system.

The leading producer responsible for the fame of Breganze abroad is Fausto Maculan, whose non-DOC wine Torcolato is a rival to the finest French Sauternes. Breganze has a lively wine festival every year in May.

BREGANZE
Az Agr Maculan* Via Castelletto 3, 36042. Tel: 0445 873733. Fax: 0445 300149. E.F.TP.WS.B.
Az Agr Villa Magna* Via Repubblica 26, 35066 Sandrigo (VI). Tel/Fax: 0444 659219. E.TP.WS.B.

For further addressess, see page 61.

Treviso - the Wine Roads

PIEVE DI SOLIGO
Le Case Bianche* Via Chisini 79. Tel: 0438 841608. Fax: 0438 980110. (Lionello Lot). 0800-1200, 1330-1800. E.F.G.TF.WS.B.

SUSEGANA
Conte Collalto* Via XXIV Maggio 1. Tel: 0438 738241. Fax: 0438 73538. (Adriano Cenedese). Mon-Fri 0800-1200, 1400-1800, Sat 0800-1200. E.G.TP.WS.B.

S STEFANO DI VALDOBBIADENE
Bisol Desiderio & Figli* Via Fol 33. Tel: 0423 900138. Fax: 0423 900577. (Elena Verri). 0800-1230, 1400-1800. Sat 0900-1200. E.G.TF.WS.B.
Ca' Salina* Via S Stefano 2. Tel: 0423 975296. Fax: 0423 975818. (Gregorio Bortolin).0900-1200, 1330-1900. E.F.G.TF.WS. (B for groups).

The *Strada del Vino Bianco*

In the soft hills between Conegliano and Valdobbiadene white wine means Prosecco. Some 3000 hectares (7500 acres) of vineyards produce this favourite aperitif of the Veneto, most often found as a dry but intensely aromatic sparkling wine. It is just as delicious in its still or sweet forms and delightful mixed with peach juice in the famous Venetian cocktail, the Bellini. While Prosecco will never have the status of a Fine Wine, it is quite impossible not to like it, and there are serious producers who make notably better versions than the mass-produced brands can provide. Look for *DOC Prosecco di Conegliano-Valdobbiadene* on the label rather than the wider appellation of DOC Prosecco. The Prosecco area actually extends far beyond the Conegliano/Valdobbiadene hills, but the product from the plains is not as good. The sub-zone of *Superiore di Cartizze* (of only about 100 hectares/250 acres) produces an expensive *cru* version of the wine, but, as usual, the quality of the producer is a better guarantee than the denomination.

The *Strada del Vino Bianco*
Back in 1966 the *Strada del Vino Prosecco*, which is the more accurate name of the *Strada del Vino Bianco*, was the first to be created in Italy. This area, at the foot of the Venetian pre-Alps, has always been a tourist area. Signposted *mescite* or *botteghe* lie along the route and serve typical regional food and wine. Conegliano, the start of the route, has a special place in the Italian wine world:

VALDOBBIADENE
Canevel Spumanti Via Cal Plandre 25. Tel: 0423 975940. Fax: 0423 975961. 0830-1230, 1400-1800. E.G.TF.WS.B.
Nino Franco Spumanti* Via Garibaldi 167. Tel: 0423 972051. Fax: 0423 975977. (Primo or Annalisa Franco). 0800-1200, 1400-1800. E.F.TF.WS.B.

VENEGAZZU DEL MONTELLO
Conte Loredan Gasparini* Via Martignago Alto. Tel: 0423 870024. Fax: 0423 620898. (Elfi Barzan). 0900-1200, 1400-1800. E.F.G.TF.WS.B.

together with San Michele all'Adige in Trentino and Asti in Piedmont, it is one of Italy's major winemaking schools.

The *Strada del Vino Bianco* begins in Conegliano's medieval castle – also the site of the town museum. The route goes west to Rua di Feletto with the remains of its ancient monastery. (Turn off at the Osteria della Guizza and go through Collalbrigo and Parè to Barriera and the Museo dell'Uomo if you want a diversion through the hills to the country life museum.) Continue to San Pietro di Feletto with its views over the hills at the Pieve (an ancient frescoed church built on a pagan site). Refrontolo looks out over the Piave valley and the hills of Montello and Grappa, all resonant names in Italy's World War I battle history.

By contrast the Mulinetto (little mill) della Croda in the nearby valley 3km (2 miles) away is a delightful place for a picnic. This area is known as the Isola del Marzemino, and produces a rare red dessert wine from the Marzemino grape; the producer Le Case Bianche is one of its few exponents. Further on towards Valdobbiadene, Pieve di Soligo is the busy capital town of the Piave area, and Col San Martino has the little frescoed church of San Vigilio with views over the Sernaglia plain below. The 12th-century Abbey of Follina is worth visiting. The Cartizze area, Prosecco's top *cru* zone, lies to the west of the road from Fol to Santo Stefano.

It is in the area from here to Valdobbiadene that most of the visitable Prosecco producers can be found.

Valdobbiadene, at the end of the Strada del Vino Bianco, lies on the slopes of the Venetian pre-Alps. This is the zone of Superiore di Cartizze, a much-prized Prosecco.

VENEGAZZU (cont.)
Montelvini Via Cal Trevigiana 51. Tel: 0423 8777. Fax: 0423 621303. (Sarah Serena). 0800-1200, 1400-1900. E.F.G.TF.WS.B.
Enoteca Vic Tesser Vini Via Spineda 8. Tel/Fax: 0423 871400. (Vic Tesser). 0800-1230, 1400-1900. E.TF.WS.

Once south of the river, there are several possibilities for wine tourism. The Montello area has some interesting stops, including the Venegazzù company, famous for its pioneering Cabernet-based wines, and nearby Vic Tesser's wine shop.

Travelling west, there is the wonderful Palladian villa at Maser, worth visiting not only for its fabulous frescoes and the beauty of its setting, but also because the owners are re-establishing its winery and re-planting its vineyards to bring the agricultural side of the estate to the fore again.

The charming hill town of Asolo, with its connections with Browning and Eleanora Duse is on everyone's itinerary, but go to Bassano del Grappa, too; you may be surprised at how much you like Italy's smartest aromatic fire-water (see pages 136-137).

Treviso
Treviso should not be missed. Only a few miles north of Venice, the bastions, canals and churches of the old town are a delight. The one-way system for traffic is incomprehensible to all but the locals, so park when you can.

Strada dei Vini del Piave: the wines
As is normal in north-east Italy the vineyards are planted with a mixture of indigenous vines – such as Verduzzo (white) and Raboso del Piave (red) – and French imports that date back to the 19th century and have become assimilated into local wine-making. These are the familiar names of Cabernet and Merlot. As always in the north-east there is a fair amount of Tocai – the white workhorse grape of the Veneto and Friuli.

The universal red is Merlot. This is an extremely easy grape to grow and vinify. It can be grown happily in the plains on

The *Strada del Vino Rosso*

an industrial scale, and the wine itself is smooth and easy to drink. Pinot Nero is rare, Pinot Bianco and Pinot Grigio make good dry white wines, and Chardonnay is ever more popular.

Strada dei Vini del Piave: the route
From Treviso head towards Roncade, whose splendid moated castle houses a well-respected winery; go to Monastier to see the superb Benedictine monastery and cross the river at Ponte di Piave. The Piave has strong associations with World War I and near Fossalta at Fagarè the Military Memorial commemorates the battle of June 1918.

From Oderzo go to San Polo di Piave. This is a famous fishery, whose gastronomic speciality is eel and red prawns in a garlic sauce. An idea of the antiquity of this tradition can be seen in the nearby church of San Giorgio at Ormelle, where a medieval fresco shows a Last Supper with red prawns.

LISON DI PORTOGRUARO
Az Agr La Braghina* Via Triestina 178. Tel: 0421 704647. Fax: 0421 287011. (Alfonso Altan). E.G.TP.WS.B.

MASER
Az Agr Villa di Maser* Via Cornuda 1. Tel: 0423 923004. Fax: 0423 923002. (Vittorio Dalle Ore). E.F.G.WS.

PIAVON DI ODERZO
Agricola Rechsteiner* Via Frassené 2. Tel: 0422 752074. Fax: 0422 752155. (Dr Hans Onno Stepski Doliwa). 0830-1230, 1430-1830. E.G.TF.WS.b.

RONCADE
Az Agr Castello di Roncade* Via Roma 141. Tel: 0422 708736. Fax: 0422 840964. (Barone Vincenzo Ciani Bassetti). E.F.G.TP.WS.

Treviso's picturesque Old Town is intersected by numerous canals.

FOOD OF THE VENETO

Polenta is absolutely universal in north-east Italy. This is a yellow maize flour which is boiled and then made into a cake that can be baked or fried; it takes a little getting used to and is truly delicious only if cooked with expertise by a local chef. It usually accompanies strong meats, such as rabbit, guinea fowl or pheasant, served with rich sauces.

Another universal dish of the Veneto is *risi bisi*, a risotto made with rice and peas, again of peasant origin. Nearly all traditional first courses are equally filling: *pasta e fagioli* (bean and pasta soup), for example, and *zuppa di trippa* (tripe soup). A legacy of pre-refrigerator days is the speciality of Vicenza, *baccalà alla vicentina*, salt cod simmered in milk and onions with the possible addition of tomatoes.

'The Rose of Chioggia' is another name for the *radicchio* plant that is used for many purposes near Treviso: in salads, grilled with pasta and even as a flavouring for Grappa.

By the Adriatic they are especially proud of their seafood. Some of the more usual fish dishes are:

Zuppa di pesce: fish soup.
Insalata di mare: mixed salad of seafood.
Seppie alla Veneziana: squid stewed in its own ink and served with pasta or with *polenta*.
Coda di Rospo: monkfish tail, usually grilled.

Strangely, the Venetians are not known so much for particular fish dishes, as for *Fegato alla Veneziana*, calves' liver cooked in butter with onions.

Continued from page 57

COLLI BERICI
Az Agr Villa Dal Ferro Lazzarini* Via Chiesa 23, 36040 San Germano dei Berici (VI). Tel: 049 8760902. Fax: 049 8759032. (Pamela and Angiola Lazzarini). TP.WS.B.

COLLI EUGANEI
Az Agr Conte Capodilista* Via Montecchia 16, 35030 Selvazzano Dentro (PD). Tel: 049 637294. Fax: 049 8055826. (Conte Giordano Emo Capodilista). Mar-Nov 0900-1200, 1430-1930. 16th-century villa. Museum. E.F.G.TP.WS.B.
Az Agr Dominio di Bagnoli* Piazza Marconi 63, 350923 Bagnoli di Sopra (PD). Tel: 049 5380008. Fax: 049 5380021. (Michela Borella). E.TP.WS.B.

Friuli-Venezia Giulia

The inhabitants of Friuli are a mixture of Slav, Latin and Teutonic traces who live peacefully in a border region which has often been the site of bitter fighting. The signs of this past are all around: Roman Aquileia, the Venetian Republic's fortress town of Palmanova; Trieste, the port of the Austro-Hungarian Empire; and the World War I battlefields at Redipúglia. But despite mass emigration after World War II and the earthquake of 1976, Friuli is one of Italy's most prosperous regions. Friuli produces an annual total of 1,300,000 hectolitres (about 30 million gallons) of wine, 54 per cent whites (mostly Tocai Friulano, Pinot Grigio, Sauvignon, Pinot Bianco and Chardonnay); the rest are reds (Merlot, Cabernet, and Refosco dal Peduncolo Rosso) and sparkling wines. The northern half is mountainous and unsuited to wine-making. In the South, however, there is an ancient tradition of viticulture which is epitomized by Friuli's most famous wine, Picolit. This is one of the great wines of the 19th century that is still produced today. The white wines of Friuli are considered by many experts to be the best in Italy.

The 4th-century mosaic floor of the ancient basilica in Aquileia is one of the glories of Friuli. It was rediscovered by accident in 1909.

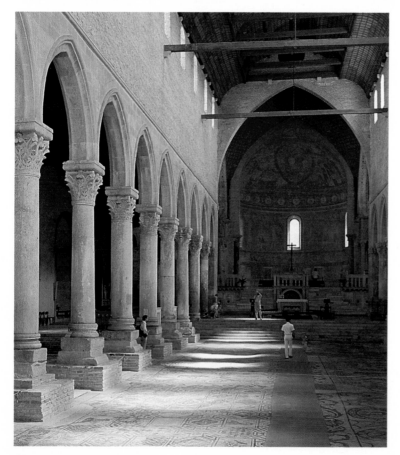

Although the wine industry here is small, the focus is on quality. New grapes, such as Cabernet, Sauvignon and Riesling, were introduced in the 19th century and today Friuli's wines have a reputation for excellence.

There are seven distinct DOC regions: Grave, Collio, Colli Orientali, Latisana, Aquileia, Isonzo, and Carso. Most of them produce the same wide range of wines, but there are notable exceptions – for example, Picolit is mainly produced in Colli Orientali.

Friuli's major problem in wine terms is the sheer number of varietals each producer cultivates. A single producer with perhaps ten hectares (25 acres) will make just as many varietal wines from individual grape varieties. And yet it is inconceivable that every producer will own ideal vineyard sites for each type of wine. Having said that, it remains true that Friuli is Italy's third most important wine region, in terms of quality, after Piedmont and Tuscany. The wine is almost all high quality, and at a commensurate price.

Friuli-Venezia Giulia

Tarcento
Nímis
Áttimis

Spilimbergo
San Daniele del Friuli

SS13

A23

R. Torre

R. Natisone

Cividale

Udine

Búttrio
Manzano

Dolegna

R. Tagliamento

Casarsa d. Delizia

SS13

Pavia di Udine

SS56

R. Isonzo

San Floriano

Cormóns

Gorizia

Codróipo
San Vito
Passariano

Pordenone

SS352

Gradisca

A28

Palmanova

A4

Redipúglia

Aquileia

SS14

Trieste

PRINCIPAL VINEYARD AREAS

Grave del Friuli

Colli Orientali del Friuli   Latisana

Collio   Aquileia

Isonzo   Carso

63

Udine, Grave and Colli Orientali

Grapes are harvested for Collavini, producers of the bestselling sparkling wine Il Grigio. Their wines are made from grapes from the Collio and Grave areas of Friuli.

GRAVE

ONTAGNANO
Az Agr Di Lenardo* Via C Battisti 1. Tel: 0432 928633. Fax: 0432 923375. 0900-1200, 1400-1800. E.T.P.WS.B.

PRATA PORDENONE
Az Agr Vigneti Le Monde*
Via Garibaldi 2, Loc Le Monde. Tel/Fax: 0434 626096. 0900-1900.
E.F.TF.WS.B.

VALERIANO
Az Agr Vicentini Orgnani*
Via Sottoplovia 2.
Tel/Fax: 0432 950107.
Mon-Fri 0830-1230, 1400-1800. Sat 0900-1200.
TP.WS.B.

Grave del Friuli: the wines
The area's name derives from the word *grave*, describing the gravelly nature of its vineyards. This is the big wine-producing area in Friuli (Pordenone has the greatest vineyard area, 5000 hectares), and white wines predominate over reds, but only just. The most common red is the Merlot, a smooth, fruity wine. Tocai Friulano is the most common white and is also the house white of every *trattoria*.

Enter Friuli on the SS13 through the charming riverside town of Sacile and the provincial capital Pordenone: if you can, take the time to see the paintings of Il Pordenone, Friuli's most famous artist, in the Duomo.

The most important factor which influenced the structure of old-established agricultural estates of this area was its annexation to Venice in the 15th century. The Tagliamento river became the eastern border of Venice's land-based territories and the supply of wood, cereals, wine, food and wool to the Serenissima became the purpose of the farming estates. Visit

Vigneti Le Monde, once the home farm of the Villa Giustinian estate, now a wine estate, and Azienda Vistorta, a typical 18th-century estate surrounded by a great park and now the seat of a 20 hectare (50 acre) winery, to get some idea of what these old agricultural complexes were like.

The Venetian Republic was formally brought to an end by Napoleon in a treaty signed just the other side of the Tagliamento at the beautiful Villa Manin, last home of the Venetian Doges.

Other places of interest in the area include Spilimbergo (with one of the finest medieval churches in Friuli), and the hill town of San Daniele, whose *prosciutto crudo* is reckoned to be even finer than the *prosciutto di Parma*.

Udine is a provincial capital with fascinating architecture, including a castle and Venetian Gothic and Renaissance buildings. It also has a wine centre, the Casa del Vino, displaying all the wines of Friuli.

Colli Orientali del Friuli

Some of the finest wines in Friuli are produced in the range of hills that forms an arc to the east of Udine. These same hills begin as Colli Orientali del Friuli (often abbreviated to COF), and become the more famous Collio Goriziano (Collio, for short) once they pass south into the province of Gorizia.

The range of COF wines is wide, 12 whites and eight reds. COF producers feel that they suffer unfairly by comparison with Collio. In some respects they are right. Most of their estates are just the other side of a provincial border to Collio, but very close geographically and producing much the same types of wines. COF also has two unique specialities: Picolit, the legendary, expensive (and not always worth it) dessert wine; and Verduzzo di Ramandolo, another dessert wine, by no means cheap, but a much better bet. COF reds are also usually bigger wines than their Collio counterparts.

From Tarcento, home of the fragrant sweet white wine, Verduzzo di Ramandolo, travel south via Nimis, Attimis, and Cividale, with its 8th-century Tempietto Longobardo, then Rosazzo, with its abbey where mixed cultivation of vines and olives has been recorded since the 12th century.

COLLI ORIENTALI (COF)

BUTTRIO
Conte d'Attimis-Maniago* Tenuta Sottomonte di Buttrio, Via Sottomonte 21. Tel: 0432 674027. Fax: 0432 674230. Mon-Fri 0800-1200, 1400-1800, Sat 0800-1200. F.TP.WS.b.
Az Agr Marina Danieli* Via Beltrame 77, Caminetto di Buttrio. Tel: 0432 673283. Fax: 0432 674421. E.G.TP.WS.b.
Az Agr Petrucco* Via Morpurgo 12. Tel/Fax: 0432 674387. 0800-1200, 1400-1800. E.TP.WS.B.

COLLOREDO DI SOFFUMBERGO
Az Agr Comelli Paolino* Tel: 0432 504973. Fax: 0432 510520. Mon-Fri 1000-1200, 1400-1800. Medieval church on site. E.TP.WS.B.

CORNO DI ROSAZZO
E Collavini*Loc Gramogliano. Tel: 0432 753222. Fax: 0432 759792. 0900-1200, 1500-1700. Museum. E.TP.WS.B.

MANZANO
Az Agr Midolini* Via Udine 40. Tel: 0432 754555. Fax: 0432 740918. 0900-1230, 1500-1830. E.G.TP.WS.B.
Az Agr Zamo' & Zamo'* Loc Rosazzo. Tel: 0432 759693. Fax: 0432 759884. Romanesque Benedictine Abbey. E.G.TP.WS.B.

S GIOVANNI AL NATISONE
Az Agr Ronco del Gnemiz* Via Ronchi 5. Tel/Fax: 0432 756238. 0900-1200, 1500-1800. E.F.G.S.TP.WS.B.

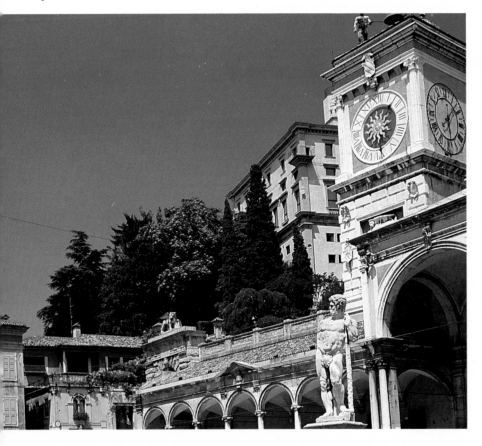

The Piazza della Libertà in Udine has an assembly of statuary dominated by an ornate clock tower dating from 1527.

Collio

Most of the old 'Garden of the Austro-Hungarian Empire', where Imperial civil servants used to holiday, is now in Slovenia. What remains is a land that produces about 1300 hectolitres (roughly 30,000 gallons) of top quality wine every year.

White wines predominate over reds by four to one. Tocai takes up one third, then, in order of size of production, Pinot Bianco, Pinot Grigio, Sauvignon, Chardonnay, Malvasia Istriana and Collio Bianco. Of the reds the most important are Merlot, Cabernet Franc and Pinot Nero.

Generally, Collio wines are bigger, rounder and fatter in taste than their counterparts from the other areas of Friuli. They are made with a slightly higher alcoholic content and are perfect wines to go with a meal.

A signposted *Strada del Vino* system was set up for the Collio in 1963. It takes in some of the most attractive vineyard-covered hill scenery in Italy, but it is also an area which saw some of the fiercest fighting of World War I – trenches are still visible in the landscape, ammunition and skeletons are still dug up in the course of vineyard cultivation.

Collio wines: the *Strada del Vino*
The wine route begins in Gorizia at the Ponte del Torrione. Gorizia itself is worth seeing for its castle, cathedral and Museum of Folklore. From Gorizia the route goes to Monte Calvario with its monument to the dead of World War I, and Oslávia, whose cemetery contains the bones of 60,000 Italian dead.

On a hill overlooking Yugoslavia is San Floriano del Collio. The 15th-century castle at the summit belongs to one of the leading producers of the Collio, Count Michele Formentini. Here, in castle buildings that his family has owned since 1520,

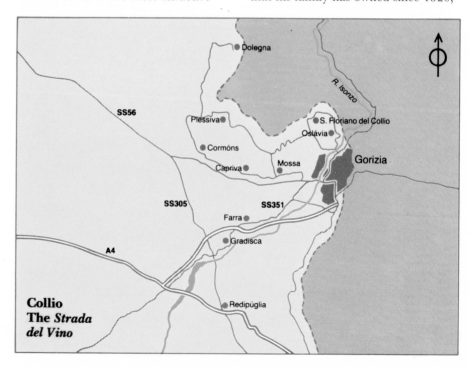

Collio
The *Strada del Vino*

Count Formentini has created a complex which combines a hotel furnished with family antiques, an Enoteca for the tasting and sale of Collio wines, and a wine museum which displays traditional winemaking artefacts.

The whole complex is surrounded by Formentini vineyards, and a 9-hole golf course. The Formentini have long been winemakers; indeed, the Furmint grape of Hungarian Tokay is said to have been named after an ancestor.

The Slovene Collio

From San Floriano the road follows the Slovene border to Plessiva. Italians can cross the border with only an identity card. In fact they are also permitted to harvest grapes from the vineyards that they still own in the Slovene Collio. But, somewhat absurdly, given the reputation of the Italian Collio, European Union law only permits the grapes so harvested to be used for the lowly *Vino da Tavola*.

Incidentally, it may well be imagined that crossing the border to Slovenia would lead the wine lover to cheaper Collio style wines produced by their Slovene neighbours. In fact, Slovenian wine can be very good, but it is not cheap.

From Plessiva go to Dolegna, with perhaps a tasting at Gianni Venica's winery. Thence to Cormons, Capriva, and Mossa. Here, before returning to Gorizia, you should visit the Regional Enoteca at Gradisca d'Isonzo. Sited in the 15th-century house of the Provveditori Veneti, the Enoteca displays wines from Friuli that have won the annual Gran Premio Noè competition. It also hosts a sparkling wine exhibition every December.

Villa Russiz is surrounded by its own vineyards in the midst of the Collio country. This is one of the most prestigious vineyard areas in Friuli.

Friuli – the Coastal Plains

The Adriatic coast of Friuli includes the three DOC wine areas of Latisana, Aquileia and, near Trieste, the Carso. Inland at the foot of the Collio are the DOC lands of the Isonzo river. Each of these areas has its own wine characteristics.

Latisana

Just over the border from the Veneto in the south-western part of Friuli is Latisana. As a town it is not particularly interesting, but as a DOC wine-making area which includes the flat land bordering the Tagliamento river on the Friuli side it is worthy of some note.

The wines are more honest than exciting, but good examples of standard Friuli favourites, such as the whites Tocai and Pinot Bianco and the red Cabernet, can be found. Two thirds of Latisana wines are red; one third is white.

A route around the vineyards might start at Latisana, go north to Varmo, east to Rivignano and descend again, via Precenicco to the seaside resort of Lignano Sabbiadoro.

Aquileia

The other side of the lagoon from Lignano is the DOC area of Aquileia. Aquileia itself was founded in 181 BC, and in Roman times became one of the principal towns of north-east Italy.

Aquileia's cathedral has important 4th-century mosaics (see photograph, page 62). Grado, the old port for Aquileia and the town the inhabitants of Aquileia fled to after the collapse of Roman rule, is also worth visiting.

Red wines predominate here. Refosco is a personal favourite, but almost the whole range of Friulan wine types can be found somewhere in the area.

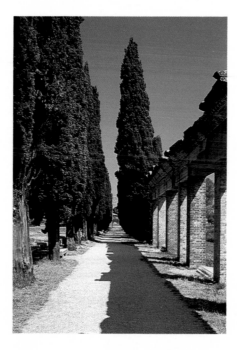

A tour of the wine-producing area might start at Cervignano del Friuli, go north to the Venetian fortress town of Palmanova, go east to San Vito al Torre and descend to Aquileia and Grado via the town of Ruda.

Carso: *Strada del Terrano*

The Carso is a relatively new DOC area created in 1985. It is named after the particular geological feature, *carsismo*, which means that water has carved out underground caverns and tunnels in the rock. The most obvious effect of this can be seen at San Giovanni al Timavo where the river suddenly bubbles up to the surface after 38km (24 miles) underground.

The two wines of the region are Malvasia Istriana and Terrano, the traditional table wine of Trieste that is reputed to be good for the blood. A *Strada del Vino* system has recently been set up with signposted roads that cover the area bounded by Monrupino, Sgonico and Duino Aurusina.

AQUILEIA
Tenuta Cà Vescovo
(Zonin) Via Case Sparse, 33050 Terzo di Aquileia. Tel: 0431 32670. Mon-Fri 0900-1200, 1400-1800 Sat 0900-1200 TF.WS.b.

Left: A cypress-lined street in old Roman Aquileia.
Below: Villa Manin at Passariano (see page 64) once the residence of Venice's last Doge, now houses an institute for research into Friuli's cultural heritage.

The Carso being an exposed strip of Italy next to Slovenia, much of it is under military jurisdiction, although tension has eased considerably since the brief period in which Slovenia was involved in the Balkan troubles.

Isonzo: *Strada del Merlot*

The DOC Isonzo area lies in the river valley at the foot of the more famous wine-producing area of the Collio hills. The Isonzo has a 40km (25 mile) *Strada del Merlot* which takes in vineyards not only of the area's best wine, Merlot, but also of the white wines Riesling Italico and Traminer.

It starts at Gradisca d'Isonzo, whose Enoteca Regionale, Enoteca La Serenissima, is a must to visit on the wine tour of Friuli (see pages 66-7), and goes on to Romans, Fratta, Medea, Borgnano, Angoris, Cormons, Brazzano, Mariano, Corona and San Lorenzo Isontino.

Excursions in this area might include the Military Museum at San Michele, near the memorial at Redipuglia, and the fortress town of Palmanova.

ISONZO
Az Agr Luisa* Via Campo Sportivo, 34070 Mariano del Friuli (GO). Tel: 0481 69680. Fax: 0481 69607. (Edi Luisa). TF.WS.

LATISANA
Az Agr Isola Augusta* Casali Isola Augusta 4, 33056 Palazzolo della Stella (UD). Tel: 0431 58046. Fax: 0431 589141. (Massimo Bassani). Museum. E.TF.WS.

TRIESTE
The Balkans begin in Trieste. Slovenes, Croats, Serbs, inhabitants of Trieste, even a few regular Italians, and a very few tourists come to this faded city fronted by the mercantile office blocks or palaces of a century ago. It all has a slightly raffish air.

There is one haven for the wine lover, especially on a Friday night. Right in the city centre, the Gran Malabar – which is so small that you have to sit outside in the corner of the square with the bar's tables and chairs – has an astonishing range of up-to-the-minute Italian wines. It was here that I tasted my first *barrique*-aged Pinot Grigio. Not bad, either. The salami was good, too.

Ask for Walter, and if you go on Friday nights, there is always a special food and wine pairing evening – one wine and one dish – and Walter's enthusiastic explanatory notes.

Gran Malabar Piazza S Giovanni 6, Trieste. Tel: 040 636226. Fri evening tastings with food.

Food of Friuli-Venezia Giulia

FOR FURTHER INFORMATION

Movimento del Turismo del Vino (Friuli-Venezia Giulia) Via Poscolle 6, 33100 Udine. Tel: 0432 509394. Fax: 0432 510180. The source of much useful information, including booklet *Itinerari del Gusto – Vini, Delizie, Bellezze in Friuli-Venezia Giulia* (also in German).

Consorzio Tutela Denominazione Origine Vini Collio Via N Sauro 9, 34071 Cormons (GO). Tel: 0481 630303. Fax: 0481 60188.

Consorzio Tutela Vini DOC Grave del Friuli c/o Camera di Commercio IAA, Corso Vittorio Emanuele 47, 33170 Pordenone. Tel: 0434 523654. Fax: 04344 21530. Useful booklet *Le Strade del Vino nel Friuli Occidentale* (also in English and German).

Consorzio Tutela Denominazione Origine Vini Colli Orientali del Friuli Via Libertà 50, 33043 Cividale del Friuli (UD). Tel: 0432 730162. Fax: 0432 730129.

OSTERIA AND FRASCA

To explore the riches of Friulan cuisine it is essential to discover the *frasca* and the *osteria*.

The *osteria* can be found in most parts of Italy, but perhaps it is here that it comes closest to the original idea of an all-day convivial meeting place where you can have a snack and glass of wine or beer at any time. There is in fact a Committee for the Defence of the Friulan *osteria*.

The *frasca*, or *mescita*, is a more impromptu and seasonal outdoor *osteria*, which mainly occurs in the two to three months around spring. Throughout the wine-producing areas *frasche* will suddenly emerge in the courtyards of farmhouses. A few rickety chairs and tables may be set outside, and you can have a plate of the typical homemade farmhouse salami and cheese products with a glass of the new season's wine for a modest sum.

FESTIVALS

Friuli
More formal festivals in Friuli include the following:
February: GRADISCA D'ISONZO: exhibition of *barrique* wines.
End March: GRADISCA D'ISONZO: week-long festival of wines of the Carso.
End April: CASARSA DELLA DELIZIA: festival of wine and Friulan folklore.
End April: AQUILEIA: wine festival.
End April: BUTTRIO: regional wine exhibition.
End April: S. FLORIANO DEL COLLIO: Tasting and Exhibition of Collio Wines.
End May: CIVIDALE DEL FRIULI: exhibition of DOC wines.
End May: GRADISCA D'ISONZO: exhibition of wines and *Gran Premio Noè*, the most important wine competition of Friuli and the one that decides which wines will be exhibited at the Enoteca Regionale at Gradisca.
July: CORMONS: wine festival.

FOOD OF FRIULI

The Friulan gastronomic tradition is a very varied one. Slav, Italian and Germanic styles are used to prepare the different foods available from the sea, hills and mountains.

The most famous food to come from Friuli is the *prosciutto crudo* of San Daniele. A recipe book published in 1450, written by Mastro Martino, the chef of the Patriarch of Aquileia, reveals how to test the readiness of this ham by plunging a knife into its centre. Nothing much has changed except that nowadays they use a fine horsebone for the same purpose. More unusual than the San Daniele ham is that of Sauris, which is another *prosciutto crudo* made from a rare breed of Friulan pig.

The Friulani are fond of soups; *jota* is the traditional soup of Trieste; *pasta con fagioli* soups are common, as is *brovada* (broth).

Rice is normally found in the coastal regions, and is used to make exquisite fish risottos. Other Friulan dishes include: *Cialzon* – each region has its own filling (rarely meat) of this traditional ravioli; *Muset* – the pasta *cotechino* is aged for about a month (hence its name, deriving from *mesetto*), and is often served in soup as a *Brovada di Muset*; and *Gulyas* – a goulash.

August: SACILE: wine festival.
August: SAN DANIELE DEL FRIULI:
Prosciutto Festival.
September: CORMONS,
RASPANOCASSACO, POVOLETTO: Festa
dell'Uva.
October: GRADISCA D'ISONZO: regional
exhibition of Grappa.

November: S. GIUSEPPE DELLA CHIUSA,
RICMANJE, S. DORLIGO DELLA VALLE:
Mostra Assaggio del Vino Nuovo, tasting
of the new season's wine.
November: ROMANS D'ISONZO: tasting,
exhibition of Collio and Isonzo wine.
December: GRADISCA D'ISONZO:
exhibition of sparkling wines.

Italians are acknowledged leaders in the field of bottle and label design. Heavy opaque bottles with deep 'punts' give a touch of special elegance to the wine. (The punt is the indentation in the centre of the base – a feature associated with Champagne and other fine wines from France.)

The Via Emilia

The Roman road of the Via Emilia unites the prosperous cities of Emilia Romagna. Every one is worth a visit, for the frescoes, statues and mosaics in their baptisteries and churches. Parma and Modena have very fine medieval and modern buildings; the Teatro Farnese in Parma and the Galleria Estense in Modena are worth seeing. Bologna is famous for its many towers, its university, and, of course, for its wonderful food. Faenza has a museum of the decorated ceramic ware that bears its name, while the ancient mosaics of Ravenna, for a time the capital of the Roman Empire after the fall of Rome, should not be missed on any account. Dante's tomb is also in Ravenna; and Garibaldi's hut in the woods, where he hid before escaping to America, can also be visited. Ferrara bears many reminders of a splendid cultural past when great Renaissance poets and painters came to the court of the Este. But there is also a special ambience to the towns and the countryside. Anyone who has seen *The Garden of the Finzi-Contini* or Bertolucci's *1900* will already have a good idea of the region's atmosphere.

Unfortunately, the region is associated with its great export, the notorious cheap party wine, Lambrusco. But, on its home ground, Lambrusco is in fact quite different. It is a great peasant wine, and it expresses in its instant earthy drinkability the first reason for drinking wine at all – for refreshment.

Wine is produced in all eight provinces of Emilia Romagna. Most comes from the large co-operatives of Forlì, Bologna and Ravenna. But the best wine comes from individual producers.

Of the most commonly found reds, the best are Gutturnio from Colli Piacentini, Lambrusco from Sorbara, and Sangiovese di Romagna. Of the whites, look out for the Sauvignon and the sparkling Malvasia from Colli di Parma, which can be both a dry aperitif wine or an excellent sweet dessert wine. Ortrugo and Pignoletto are the latest discoveries for insiders· in the wine world. Albana has long been criticized as an unworthy DOCG, but is now finding its true vocation as a delicious *passito* wine. These wines are some of Italy's best-kept secrets.

The wines of Romagna are promoted by the Ente Tutela dei Vini Romagnoli, which uses as its trademark the bearded figure of a Passatore, the gentleman bandit of the 18th and 19th centuries, part of the folklore of the once lawless Romagna region.

72

PRINCIPAL VINEYARD AREAS

Gutturnio dei Colli Piacenti

Lambrusco

Lambrusco Salamino

Lambrusco di Sorbara

Lambrusco Grasparossa

Sangiovese di Romagna

Albana di Romagna

Trebbiano di Romagna

Wines of the Via Emilia

PIACENZA

VAL D'ARDA

Az Agr Vit Buffalora
29020 Rezzano, Carpaneto
Piacentino (PC). Tel/Fax:
0523 850123. (Luigi
Montesissa). 0800-1200,
1400-2000. T.P.WS.B.
Az Agr Luretta Paolini di
Bradasco 3, 29010
Vernasca (PC). Tel/Fax:
0523 895465. (Carla Asti).
0900-1730. E.F.T.P.WS.B.
**Az Agr Vitivinicola
Pusterla*** 29010 Vigolo
Marchese (PC). Tel/Fax:
0523 896105. (Giovanna or
Giorgio Freschi or Eugenio
Gandolfi). Mar-Oct 1000-
1900. Historic cellars.
E.F.G.T.P.WS.B.

VAL NURE

Az Agr La Tosa* Loc La
Tosa, 29020 Vigolzone
(PC). Tel/Fax: 0523
870727. (Stefano
Pizzamiglio). 0800-1200,
1400-1800. Small museum.
E.F.T.P.WS.B.

VAL TIDONE

Castello di Luzzano*
Az Agr M & G Fugazza,
27040 Rovescala (PV). Tel:
0523 863277. Fax: 0523
865909. (Giovanna
Fugazza). 0800-1200,
1400-1800. Roman
archeological remains on
site, *agriturismo*, organized
wine tours. E.F.T.P.WS.B.

The Via Emilia was constructed by the Romans in the late 2nd century BC. It stretches from Piacenza in the north to Rimini on the Adriatic coast. It was, and still is, a great commercial highway.

Piacenza

The town of Piacenza itself was badly damaged in World War II. Its importance in the wine world lies in the wines produced in the Colli Piacentini hills that line the valleys fanning out to the west and south. Most Colli Piacentini wines – even the reds – can be still, semi-sparkling, sparkling, sweet or dry, depending on how the producer wishes to make them. The locals prefer their wines to have a slight sparkle, *frizzantino*, to accentuate the fruit and freshness of young vintages. Perhaps the most interesting wines for the visitor are the honest, very quaffable reds, Bonarda and Barbera, and the delicate whites Ortrugo and Malvasia.

Gutturnio, a serious wine drinker's red wine, definitely not sparkling, is a blend of Barbera and Bonarda and named after the Roman drinking vessel found near Piacenza in 1878 that has become the symbol of its producers. Just to add to the plethora of wines in this area, many serious producers are now using Chardonnay, Sauvignon, Cabernet and Pinot Noir, the international varieties, with increasing success. The aromatic qualities of Sauvignon and Pinot Noir particularly come out well in an area used to making aromatic wines.

Piacenza – the wine roads

Visiting producers in the Colli Piacentini means exploring the valleys that lie to the south of the city. From west to east these are:
Val Tidone: Go through Borgonovo with its castle to begin the vineyard area leading to Ziano, the capital town of Val

Tidone with more than 750 registered wine growers. Go south to the impressive fortress of Olgisio or follow the hills from Vicobarone to Fornello or Luzzano to the west.
Val Trebbia: The Trebbia valley has its own tongue-twisting white wine, Trebbianino, and was described by Hemingway as one of the most beautiful valleys in Italy. The main road, the SS45, is the old road to Liguria and is dotted with castles that used to defend it, such as Ancarano, Montechiaro and Bobbio. The basilica of Bobbio is the resting place of Saint Colomba of Ireland.
Val Nure: If you have a taste for medieval pastiche, visit Grazzano Visconti to see the Victorian Medieval Gothic village and try the wines in the Enoteca there. The valley has its own sparkling white wine, Valnure, and is the site of several leading wine companies.
Val d'Arda: Visit Castell'Arquato to see a delightful medieval fortified town and to taste wines in the regional Enoteca. The Arda valley has a sweet sparkling wine called Monterosso, which, as usual with the local wines of Colli Piacentini, is a variation on the theme of a grape mix using Ortrugo, Malvasia and Trebbiano grapes.

Parma, Reggio Emilia and Modena

The town of Parma is well worth a visit, but again it is the hills, the Colli di Parma, that provide the wine. This is an area which is attracting increasing interest for its whites, particularly Sauvignon and Malvasia. The *frizzantino* versions are the standard white wine aperitifs in local bars. Reggio Emilia is a surprisingly attractive and unspoilt town, full of wonderfully operatic piazzas and impressive churches. The wines of the area are Lambrusco Reggiano, from the plains, and Bianco di Scandiano, from the hills to the south.

Modena is a busy commercial city that seems to mix a modern sense of purpose with a stately architectural background. This is where the other two Lambrusco wines, Lambrusco Salamino di Santa Croce and Lambrusco di Sorbara, come from.

Lambrusco

The actual denomination of Lambrusco does not seem to matter for quality purposes, the important point is to find a serious producer. The bubbles are usually the product of tank fermentation, but there are still a few producers who make the costly bottle-fermented version, which can be very good. As usual, good local Lambrusco is the ideal accompaniment to good local foods.

Lambrusco is, of course, always red, and either dry or *amabile* (medium-dry). The sweet red, white and rosé versions that can be found in supermarkets are as far away from real Lambrusco as British ice-cream is from Italian.

Colli Bolognesi

Bologna is not really on the tourist map, which makes it a good place to visit. The National Art Gallery is excellent. But the food is so good that it outshines the wine; to find wine interest, go to the Colli Bolognesi, the hills to the south of the city. Colli Bolognesi wines include Cabernet, Barbera and Merlot reds; and Pignoletto, Sauvignon, Riesling, Chardonnay and Pinot Bianco whites. Pignoletto produced by the Gaggioli company is one of my personal favourites, as is the Cabernet Sauvignon from Terre Rosse.

The wine route in the gentle Colli Bolognesi starts at Zola Predosa, goes on to Bazzano (castle), then to Monteveglio (medieval town complex) and Savigno by the old Roman Via Claudia; then the road loops back towards Bologna via San Chierlo (visit the church of San Biagio in the Poggio district) and the 12th-century Abbey of San Fabiano near Calderino.

Wines of the Romagna

The principal wines of the Romagna are: Sangiovese di Romagna, a light and uncomplicated red; Trebbiano di Romagna, a simple white wine; Cagnina and Pagadebit (this last one literally providing big enough crops to 'pay the bills'); and the controversial Albana di Romagna.

Albana was the first Italian white wine to gain the prestigious DOCG recognition (see pages 10-11), but no-one quite knew why. In the hands of most producers it was, and is, an undistinguished wine, at least in its dry version. What has emerged, however, as a result of the stringency of DOCG regulations, is that *passito* Albana di Romagna is an exceptional dessert wine. Try the Tre Monti version for a wine that tastes of apricots and mango.

VAL TREBBIA

Az Agr La Stoppa* Loc Ancarano, 29029 Rivergaro (PC). Tel: 0523 958159. Fax: 0523 956085. (Angela and Elena Pantaleoni). 0830-1230, 1400-1900. E.F.TP.WS. (B for groups or outside office hours).

Az Agr Marchese Malaspina* C.da Borgoratto 26, 29022 Bobbio (PC). Tel: 0523 936048. Fax: 0383 60195. (Guido Bellocchio). TP.WS.B.

PARMA

Az Agr Monte delle Vigne* Via Costa 27, 43036 Ozzano Taro (PR). Tel: 0521 809105. Fax: 0521 809915. (Elisabetta Oppici). 0900-1300, 1500-1900. Also producers of cheese and Parma ham. E.F.TP.WS.B.

REGGIO EMILIA

Az Agr Venturini-Baldini* Via F Turati 42, 42020 Roncolo di Quattro Castella (RE). Tel: 0522 887080. Fax: 0522 888141. (Daniela Brindani). 0800-1200, 1400-1800. On Terre di Matilde di Canossa route. E.F.TP.WS.B.

Brisighella, in the Romagna, celebrates its history with a two-week medieval fair each summer.

COLLI BOLOGNESI

Tenuta Bonfiglio* Via Cassola 23, 40050 Monteveglio (BO). Tel/Fax: 051 831813. (Maria Luisa Vannozzi). 0800-1900. E.G.S.TP.WS.B.

Tenuta Bonzara* Via San Chierlo 37a, 40050 Monte S Pietro (BO). Tel/Fax: 051 225772. (Francesco Lambertini). 0830-1200, 1400-1800. Agricultural life museum, restaurant, *agriturismo*. E.F.TP.WS.B.

Az Agr Gaggioli* Vigneto Bagazzana, Via Raibolini 55, 40069 Zola Predosa (BO). Tel/Fax: 051 753489. (Maria Letizia Gaggioli). 0800-1200. E.TP.WS.B.

Vigneto delle Terre Rosse* Via Predosa 83, 40069 Zola Predosa (BO). Tel/Fax: 051 755845. (Elisabetta Vallania). 0800-1200, 1430-1800. E.F.G.TP.WS.B.

Az Agr Vallona* S. Andrea 203, Loc Fagnano, Castello Serravalle (BO). Tel: 051 6703058/ 6703066. Fax: 051 6703333. (Maurizio Vallona). TP.WS.B.

IMOLA

Az Agr Tre Monti* Via Lola 3, Loc. Bergullo, 40026 Imola (BO). Tel: 0542 657116. Fax: 0542 657122. (David Navacchia). 0800-2000. E.TP.WS.

Imola and Faenza

The little town of Dozza, just outside Imola, is fundamental to any wine tour in Emilia-Romagna. Here, the regional Enoteca, the information centre for Emilia-Romagna wines, occupies the old castle whose storerooms provide perfect cellar conditions for wine display. The town has also come to prominence because of the custom of decorating the houses in the narrow town centre with pictures painted on to their walls by modern artists.

From Dozza it is only a short distance to Imola, famous for its race-track but relatively undiscovered for its delightful Renaissance and 18th-century architecture.

A diversion through the hills goes through the spa town of Riolo Terme to medieval Brisighella. Three outcrops of rock with a clock tower dating back to 1290 and a 14th-century castle dominate the town. The wine route ends in Faenza, with its International Ceramics Museum.

Forlì

The hills south of Forlì offer two destinations. Modigliana, the home of the Castelluccio winery is reached via Terra del Sole, a fortified complex built by Cosimo de' Medici with some interesting Renaissance *palazzi* and a Museum of Country Life. The other destination is Bertinoro, the 'balcony of Romagna', further east towards Cesena, but in the hills overlooking the plain towards Ravenna. It has a medieval centre, an Enoteca, and, just outside the town, lies Fattoria Paradiso, providing a unique opportunity to sample wine and admire vintage cars at the same time.

Ravenna

Surprisingly enough, there are wines produced along the Adriatic coast in the area called Bosco Eliceo around Ravenna. They are difficult to find and the effort is probably better spent feasting the eyes on the glorious mosaics of Ravenna itself in the Basilica of San Vitale and the church of Sant'Apollinare Nuovo.

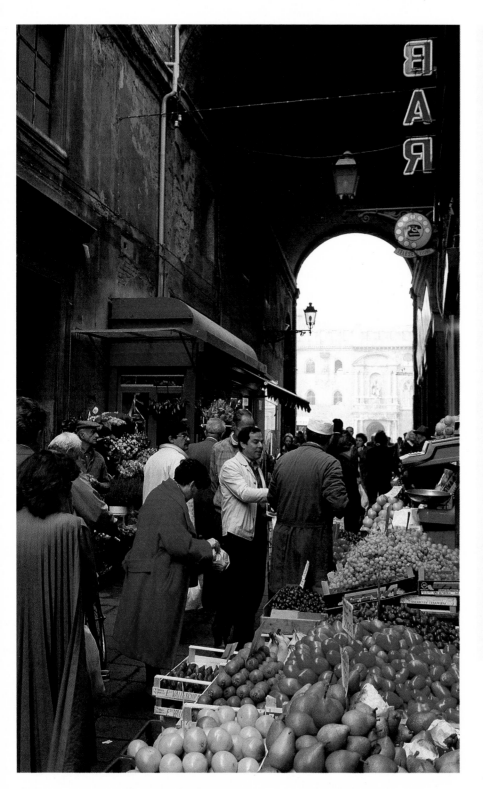

DOZZA
Enoteca Regionale Emilia-Romagna Rocca Sforzesca. Tel: 0542 678089. Fax: 0542 678073. Tue-Fri 1000-1200, 1500-1800. Information centre for all Emilia-Romagna wines.

FAENZA

Fattoria Camerone* Via Biancanigo 1485, 48014 Castel Bolognese (RA). Tel: 0546 50434. Fax: 0546 656146. (Dr Giuseppe Marabini). 0800-1200, 1400-2000. E.F.G.TP.WS.B.
Conti Leone* Corso Matteotti 16, 48018 Faenza (RA) Tel: 0546 642149. Fax: 0546 642222. (Leone Conti). 1400-1700. E.TP.WS.B.
Az Agr Trerè* Via Casale 19, Monticoralli, 48018 Faenza (RA). Tel/Fax: 0546 47034. (Morena Trerè). 0830-1200, 1430-1830. E.F.TP.WS.b.

FORLÌ

Castelluccio* Via Tramonto 15, 47015 Modigliana (FO). Tel/Fax: 0546 92486 (Gian Matteo Baldi). 1000-1600. E.TP.WS.B.
Fattoria Paradiso* Via Palmeggiana 285, 47032 Bertinoro (FO). Tel: 0543 445044. Fax: 0543 444224. (Marco Lorenzini). 0900-1200, 1500-1900. Vintage car museum. *Taverna*, nr Cà da Bè in Bertinoro and Borgo Medioevale. E.F.S.TP.WS.B.

Left: A fruit and vegetable market in one of Bologna's characteristically tall arcades. In addition to being the gastronomic capital of Italy, Bologna also boasts the oldest university in Europe, dating from the 11th century.

Food of the Via Emilia

Bologna is Italy's gastronomic capital; all Italians will tell you that their gastronomic dream is to go to one of the better restaurants of Bologna. A simple plateful of *Tortelloni alla Bolognese* served with just a flake of fresh local butter and some freshly grated parmesan, can make the most memorable of meals.

You don't have to be a foodie to realize when you arrive in Bologna that the locals have got it right. Even the pizzas are adorned with fragrant veils of pink Parma ham, or thin shavings of Parmesan cheese. And the *tortelloni*, well, even the Italians roll their eyes with anticipated pleasure when you mention that you found the most melting egg pasta. Not to mention the fillet steak with Balsamic Vinegar sauce. Or the delicious apricot sweetness of an Albana *passito* dessert wine. Not for nothing is Bologna La Dotta ('the Learned') also called Bologna La Grassa ('the Fat').

There are four products that the Emilia-Romagnans tempt us with: the wines, of course; Parmesan cheese, the finest of all the *grana* cheeses; Parma ham, the sweetest and pinkest of all cured hams; and Balsamic Vinegar, the elixir of Reggio Emilia and Modena.

Parmesan

Parmigiano-Reggiano is the authentic parmesan cheese. There are other hard cheeses; *grana padano* from near Milan is the nearest competitor, but it is not as good. Parmesan is made in a totally natural and centuries-old way that involves the addition of nothing more than rennet to the milk from cows from a strictly delimited area. The long 18 months' ageing and the grazing and micro-organisms specific to the high pastures contribute to the unique taste and cooking qualities of the cheese. Ageing can be as long as three years, two is ideal for most purposes.

Parmigiano can be bought direct from the makers at any of the small *caseifici* cheese factories in the area (there are several between Reggio Emilia and the hills). When buying the cheese, examine it carefully. It should be a uniform moist but pale amber colour and should be without any tell-tale signs of dryness, such as white patches or a white rim next to the rind. Taste it – it should dissolve in granular smoothness in the mouth and have a nutty and slightly salty taste.

Parma ham

Since Roman times the valleys south-west of Parma have been famous for the production of hams. The wind that dries and sweetens genuine Parma ham blows pure in this region.

Humble pie

There is a phrase in Italian about having to 'go to Canossa', which is roughly equivalent to being compelled to 'eat humble pie'. This recalls the incident in the early 11th century when the Holy Roman Emperor, Henry IV, was forced to humble himself before Pope Gregory VII by going to Canossa and waiting barefoot in the snow for four days before being granted absolution.

The castle at Canossa is now the centre of a sign-posted trail (the Percorsi Matildici) in the hills to the south of Reggio Emilia, dotted with hamlets, towers and churches.

Balsamic Vinegar

Everyone has heard of Balsamic Vinegar, the rich sweet viscous liquid, aged in a series of barrels of differing woods and decreasing size in the vinegar lofts of Modena and Reggio Emilia.

One drop fills the room with perfume; over fifty years old it is used as an after dinner drink, literally an elixir. This is the stuff of legends; unfortunately, it is rarely the liquid you find, and it really does cost a lot of money. Necessarily so. There are, in fact, two types of Balsamic Vinegar, one rare and expensive and the product of years of careful ageing, the other a creation for the mass market.

Unless the Balsamic Vinegar name contains the word *tradizionale*, assume the worst.

Aceto Balsamico Tradizionale di Modena, or di Reggio Emilia, are the genuine products.

MODENA
Az Agr Pedroni* Via Risaia 2, 41015 Nonantola. Tel: 059 549019. Fax: 059 542514. 0800-1100, 1700-2000. Restaurant, *aceto balsamico tradizionale.* TP.WS.B.

Parmigiano-Reggiano (Parmesan) cheese is aged for at least 18 months after first being formed.

The selected hams, from pigs weighing about 150 kilos (330 pounds), have a finished cured weight of about seven kilos (15 pounds). They are salted with the minimum salt possible and hung up for seven to nine months in carefully controlled conditions that include the occasional blast of fresh air.

The hams are tested, traditionally with a bone spike, to check for thorough curing. Those that pass the quality control are given the stamp of the Ducal Crown of Parma.

Other local foods

Coppa: this is a dried and cured meat made from the neck and shoulders of the pig. It is eaten thinly sliced with bread and butter.

Felino: reckoned to be the finest salami of Emilia Romagna but hard to locate.

Zampone di Modena: stuffed pig's trotter; can now be bought vacuum-packed in many delicatessens.

Mortadella: the huge and soft spiced pink sausage made from pork (all parts), now so famous as to have its cut-price imitations. The genuine product is very good. As is the case with most sausages, it is probably best not to ponder too much on the exact ingredients.

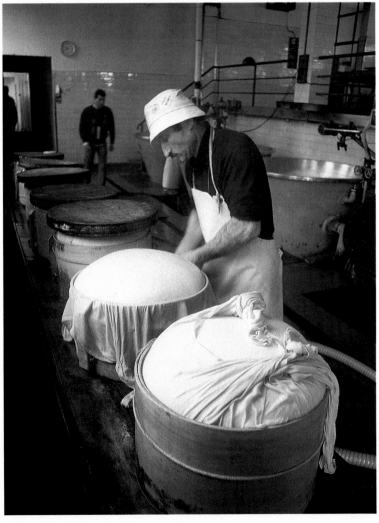

Tuscany

or many of its visitors, Tuscany is Italy. Indeed this is the geographic and cultural centre of Italy and once, from 1864 to 1871, it was the political centre too. But most of all Tuscany is Grand Tour country: few cities in the world can compare with Florence for its wealth of art and brilliant architecture; Siena is smaller, but extraordinarily rich in medieval treasures; and the little hilltop town of San Gimignano is a perfectly preserved picture of medieval life. Less obvious are the industries of Tuscany: the marble of Carrara, Prato's textiles, Val d'Elsa furniture, Florentine leather goods, jewellery, and so on. Tourism is still central, of course. The most dynamic wine producers in Tuscany tend to be outsiders, including many foreigners and escapees from Milan, who, having become enchanted with the dream of Tuscan life themselves, are keen to welcome visitors and share the experience. Tourism is such a integral part of Tuscan life anyway that it is no surprise that the *Movimento del Turismo del Vino* was born in Tuscany and finds its keenest exponents here – good news for the wine tourist.

The dome with a view is a technical and artistic masterpiece by the early Renaissance architect Brunelleschi. It crowns Florence's cathedral.

Wine tourism in Tuscany is well developed, but, as in the rest of Italy, not yet standardized. At its most basic, the establishment of a rapport with a local wine producer can lead to a bucolic afternoon of never-ending tasting and increasingly fluent Italian.

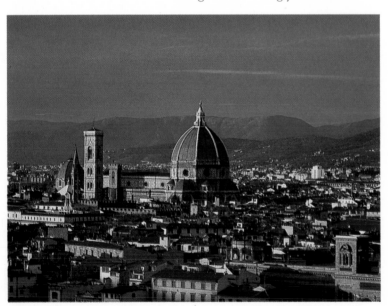

Buying wine by the case from the *fattoria* door is a long-established part of Italian life, but what to do about the casual visitor who would like to taste the wine? This is a new development, and some producers have tried to establish a norm for visitors.

Most Tuscan wineries have evolved a range of solutions. Some have kiosks on the main road selling their wine. A few are happy for anyone to arrive at almost any time. Many provide a very attractive type of tasting and snack service whereby a small group of visitors can book a tasting of the estate's wines with *spuntini*, snacks of local bread, cheese and salami, for a set fee.

If some wineries specify a charge for tasting, this is largely to put off *curiosi* (time-wasters) and to ensure that visitors are serious. It is rarely much more than the cost of the bottles opened and a little bit for the producer's time, and may be forgotten entirely if wine is subsequently purchased. Winemaking is a business, after all.

A15

S62

S63

R. Serchio

S12

La
Spezia

Carrara

S1

A12

Massa

COLLINE
LUCCHESI

MONTECARLO

A11

Lucca

S64

S12

Pisa

Carmignano

CARMIGNANO

Empoli

R. Arno

A11

A1

Pistoia

S65

S67

A11

CHIANTI
RUFINA

Rufina

POMINO

Florence

Pontassieve

S71

Impruneta

S429

R. Elsa

Greve

S69

Arezzo

R. Era

Certaldo

Livorno

A12

VERNACCIA DI
SAN GIMIGNANO

CHIANTI
CLASSICO

S1

S. Gimignano

CHIANTI

Montescudaio

S68

R. Cécina

S222

Siena

S71

MONTESCUDAIO

Bolgheri

S541

S2

S326

BOLGHERI

Buonconvento

Montepulciano

VINO NOBILE DI
MONTEPULCIANO

Montalcino

Pienza

BRUNELLO DI
MONTALCINO

S1

S223

A1

Elba

S1

R. Ombrone

ELBA

Grosseto

Scansano

Pitigliano

MORELLINO DI
SCANSANO

BIANCO DI
PITIGLIANO

S2

Parrina

PARRINA

S1

From Pisa to Florence

been good. Fattoria del Buonamico set the example in the area for quality wines that others have now followed.

The wine route
The wine route leaves Lucca going north on the SS12 up the Serchio valley towards Bagni di Lucca and swings east towards Matraia (Fattoria Colle Verde), Tofori (Fattoria Maionchi), Gragnano (Tenuta Spadaro) and then Montecarlo. There are several imposing villas in the area, particularly Villa Reale at Marlia, Villa Torrigiani at Camigliano and Villa Mansi at Segromigno.

Lucca retains its medieval street plan, safely protected from development by its massive city walls

COLLI FIORENTINI

Fattoria Montalbano* 50060 Donnini (FI). Tel: 055 8652158. Fax: 055 8652270. 0900-1200, 1500-1900. E.G.TF.WS.
Fattoria Montellori* Via Pistoiese 5, 50054 Fucecchio (FI). Tel: 0571 260641. Fax: 0571 242625. 0900-1200, 1500-1800. E.G.TP.WS.b.
Fattoria San Vito in Fior di Selva* Via S Vito 32, 50050 Malmantile (FI). Tel: 0571 51411. Fax: 0571 51405. 0900-1700. E.F.G.TP.WS.B.

COLLINE LUCCHESI

Fattoria Colle Verde* Loc Castello, 55010 Matraia (LU). Tel: 0583 402310. Fax: 0583 402256. 1000-1200, 1400-1800. E.F.S.TF.WS.b
Tenuta Maria Teresa* 55060 S Martino in Vignale (LU). Tel: 0583 394412. Fax: 0583 394345. Sat 1000-1300. E.TF.WS. (B other times).
Fattoria Maionchi* 55010 Tofori (LU). Tel: 0583 978194/0330 604012. Fax: 0583 978345. 0900-1200, 1400-1800. E.F.TF.WS.b.

Despite the growth in direct flights to Florence, for many people Pisa is still the gateway to Tuscany. Towns in between tend to be ignored, which benefits those who do make the effort to visit them.

Lucca
An independent city state up until the creation of the Napoleonic Kingdom of Italy, Lucca retains much physical evidence of its history. A quadrilateral street layout shows its Roman origins: the old Roman amphitheatre has been magically transformed into houses, but in exactly the same shape, and the walls that kept the Medici out were always too massive to remove.

The two DOC denominations of the area are Colline Lucchesi, coming from the arc of hills to Lucca's north; and Montecarlo, from the area surrounding the little hilltop medieval village about 15km (10 miles) east of Lucca.

Red Colline Lucchesi wine is like Chianti; the white is based on Trebbiano and 'does not travel'. Montecarlo wines are more interesting. The whites allow for all sorts of exciting grapes to complement the standard Trebbiano (from Sémillon to Sauvignon), and the reds have always

Carmignano

Just to the west of Florence, almost the last stretch of real countryside before the suburban sprawl begins, is Monte Albano and the Carmignano area.

Carmignano is a red DOCG wine, and it is almost entirely unknown, even in Italy. It has an illustrious past, having been codified by decree in 1716 when Grand Duke Cosimo III defined its exact production zone, more or less corresponding to the enclosed Medici estate known as the Barco Reale. The link is acknowledged today with the wine called Barco Reale, in effect a second wine to the full-blown Carmignano.

The second boost to Carmignano was the fact that the Medici introduced many experimental vines on their estate, including the all-important Cabernet Sauvignon from France. This enabled modern producers of Carmignano legitimately to build in a certain component of Cabernet in the official DOC for the wine, right from its promulgation in 1975.

Carmignano is in the hands of a very few producers, reflecting its aristocratic past. Visiting the area is also an opportunity to see some fine Tuscan villas. Fattoria di Artimino has a modern and architecturally undistinguished winery, but the villa itself is a splendid Medici creation and contains an Etruscan museum of locally found remains. There is another, more spectacular Medici villa, open to the public, at Poggio a Caiano.

Carmignano itself is worth a visit to see Pontormo's *Visitation* in the church of San Michele. Nearby Capezzana has the estate of Carmignano's leading producers, the Contini Bonacossi family at Tenuta di Capezzana, who have carried the Cabernet theme of local wines to its logical conclusion with their Ghiaie della Furba, a Bordeaux blend of Cabernet Sauvignon, Cabernet Franc, and Merlot. While in this area, it is worth visiting Vinci, to see the museum dedicated to models of the inventions of the great Leonardo da Vinci, and to visit his birthplace at Anchiano.

COLLINE LUCCHESI (cont.)

Fattoria La Poggiola* Via Treggiaia 13, 531030 Serravalle Pistoiese (PT). Tel/Fax: 0573 51071. 1500-1900. *Agriturismo.* E.F.TF. (TP for groups). WS.b.

Tenuta Gaetano Spadaro* Via dei Pieroni 76, 55010 Gragnano (LU). Tel/Fax: 0583 974147. 0900-2400. E.G.TP.WS.B.

MONTECARLO

Fattoria del Buonamico* Via Prov. di Montecarlo 43. Tel/Fax: 0583 22038. 0830-1230, 1400-1900. E.F.TF.WS. (B Sat pm, hols).

Fattoria Il Poggio* Via S Piero 39. Tel/Fax: 0583 22088 G.TF.WS.B.

Fattoria Michi* Via S Martino 34. Tel/Fax: 0583 22011. 0800-1230, 1330-1830. E.TF.WS. (B for food).

CARMIGNANO

Fattoria di Artimino* Viale Papa Giovanni XXIII, 50040 Artimino (FI). Tel: 055 8792051. Fax: 055 8792044. 0800-1200, 1400-1700. E.TF.WS.B.

Fattoria di Bacchereto* Via Fontemorana 179, 50040 Bacchereto (Prato). Tel/Fax: 055 8717191.

Tenuta di Capezzana* Via Capezzana 100, 50042 Carmignano (Prato). Tel: 055 8706005 Fax: 055 8706673. Mon-Fri 1500-1700. E.TP.WS.B.

Fattoria Il Poggiolo* 50042 Carmignano (PO). Tel: 055 8711242. Fax: 055 8711252. 0800-1200, 1400-1800. E.TF.WS.B.

The Coast of Tuscany

COLLINE PISANE

Az Agr Bruno Moos* Via
Pier Capponi 98, 56030
Soiana (PI). Tel/Fax: 0587
654180. E.F.G.S.TE.WS.B.

Fattoria Badia di Morrona*
Via di Badia 8, 56030
Terriciola (PI). Tel: 0587
658505. Fax: 0587 655127.
TF.WS.b.

Fattoria Uccelliera* Via
Pontita 26, 56043 Fauglia
(PI) Tel: 050 662747. Fax:
050 662663. 1000-1800. TP
(for groups). WS.B.

MONTESCUDAIO

Fattoria Poggio Gagliardo*
Loc Poggio Gagliardo. Tel:
0586 630661. Fax: 0586
685960. 0900-1200, 1500-
1900. E.F.G.TE.WS.b.

BOLGHERI

Podere Grattamacco*
57022 Castagneto Carducci
(LI). Tel: 0565 763840. Fax:
0565 763217. E.F.TE.WS.B.

**Antica Fabbrica di
Liquori Emilio Borsi** Via
Garibaldi 5a, 57022
Castagneto Carducci (LI).
Tel: 0565 766017. 0930-
1300, 1630-2400. Liqueurs.

Frantoio Fonte di Foiano
Loc Fonte di Foiano, 57022
Castagneto Carducci (LI).
Tel: 0565 763442. Mon-Sat
1630-2000, Sun 0800-1200.
Olive oil tasting.

VAL DI CORNIA

Az Agr Bulichella*
Loc.Bulichella, 57028
Suvereto (LI). Tel: 0565
829892. Fax: 0565 829553.
0800-1800. E.F.TE.WS.

Gualdo del Re* Loc Notri
77, 57028 Suvereto (LI).
Tel/Fax: 0565 829888.
0800-2000 TF.WS.b.

Podere San Luigi* Via
dell'Arsenale 16, 57025
Piombino (LI) Tel: 0565
30380. Fax: 0565 20812.
E.F.TE.WS.b.

The suggestion that good wines can
come from Tuscany's coastal hinterland
would have seemed ridiculous only a
few years ago, if it had not been for
Italy's most famous red wine, Sassicaia,
which comes from Bolgheri (and here
everyone has to consult an atlas).

Colline Pisane
The hills south-east of Pisa on the
other side of the Arno form one of the
seven Chianti zones. However, the few
producers of real quality in the area
often make more interesting wines
outside the limits of Chianti DOCG
regulations than inside.

Montescudaio
Here you find more Chianti-formula
reds and Trebbiano-based whites, once
again redeemed by the efforts of
individual producers. The estates of
the wine producers lie along the
Cecina river and around Casale,
Guardistallo and Montescudaio.

Bolgheri
Why has it taken so long for the success of
Sassicaia to be emulated? Cabernet
Sauvignon and Merlot seem to flourish in
this part of Tuscany and Bordeaux blends
(a mixture of the two) are more successful
than Sangiovese-based Chianti look-alikes.

The aristocratic estates of the
region take in vast areas of scrubby
hinterland between the coast and the
hills. These used to produce a dull local
rosé until Antinori's winemaker,
Giacomo Tachis, was brought in to
decide what to do with the Cabernet
Sauvignon vines brought back from
France and planted on the Incisa della
Rochetta estate at Bolgheri (closed to
the public). The result was Sassicaia,
which has been an enormous success.

Of the local estates in the Bolgheri
area, probably Podere Grattamacco is

the most welcoming and increasingly
impressive. Two unusual visits in the
area might be to the beautifully clean
olive oil mill at Fonte di Foiano and to
Borsi, the hand-crafted liqueur *bottega*
in Castagneto Carducci itself.

The south
The coastal hinterland of Southern
Tuscany is rich in Etruscan remains.
Populonia, now a fishing village, but once
Puplona, an important Etruscan trading
centre, is very impressive. If Etruscan
remains fascinate you, then be sure to go
to Vetulonia, between Grosseto and
Massa Marittima, Tarquinia and Sovana,
down near Pitigliano.

Pitigliano, in the heart of Etruscan Tuscany, is well known for its white wine.

Southern Tuscany has ceased to be just border land and has acquired its own identity, ever since the draining of the Maremma swamps finally allowed the eradication of malaria in the area earlier this century.

The wines, from Val di Cornia near Massa Marittima to Morellino, Parrina and Pitigliano in the far south, are all variations on a theme. The reds are based on Sangiovese, Tuscany's traditional red grape. What gives them their local identity are the other grapes that are part of the final blend. Morellino di Scansano, for example, southern Tuscany's most important red, can be made as 100 per cent Sangiovese.

But other producers who use it put Morellino's spicy, accessible style down to the local practice of blending with Alicante, a variation of the better-known Grenache from France.

The whites are based on Trebbiano. Here again the final character of the wine will depend on the other grapes used to give the bland base grape some character. Bianco di Pitigliano, for example, is mostly Trebbiano but can include percentages of Chardonnay, Greco, Grechetto, Malvasia, Riesling, Verdello, Sauvignon, and Pinot Bianco.

MAREMMA

Az Agr Erik Banti Loc Fosso dei Molini, 58054 Scansano (GR). Tel: 0564 508006. Fax: 0564 508019. 0830-1230, 1400-1730. E.F.G.Danish. TF.WS.b.

Moris Farms* Fattoria Poggetti, Loc Cura Nuova, 58020 Massa Marittima (GR). Tel: 0566 919135. Fax: 0566 919380. 0800-1200, 1600-1900. E.TF.WS.b.

Tenuta La Parrina* Loc Parrina, Albinia, 58010 Grosseto. Tel/Fax: 0564 862636. 0800-1300, 1500-1800. E.G.TF.WS.B.

Rufina

Numbers in square brackets refer to map (inset, opposite).

NIPOZZANO
Castello di Nipozzano*
Loc Nipozzano. Tel/Fax:
055 8311050. 0900-1800.
E.F.G.TP.WS.B. **[7]**

POMINO
Castello di Pomino*
Loc Pomino. Tel/Fax: 055
8318810. 0900-1800.
E.F.G.TP.WS.B. **[8]**

PONTASSIEVE
**Tenuta Marchese Gondi
Fattoria dei Bossi*** Via
dello Stracchino 32. Tel: 055
8317830. Fax: 055 8364008.
1500-1800. E.F.TP.WS.B. **[5]**
**Fattoria Castello del
Trebbio*** Via S Brigida 9,
Loc S Brigida. Tel: 055
8300051. Fax: 055 8300502.
0900-1200, 1400-1800.
E.G.TF.WS.B. **[4]**
Fattoria di Selvapiana*
Loc Selvapiana 43. Tel: 055
8369848. Fax: 055 8316840.
0900-1900. E.G.TF.WS.b. **[6]**

RUFINA
Az Agr Colognole* Via
Palagio 15, Loc Colognole.
Tel: 055 8319870. Fax: 055
8319605. *Agriturismo.* 0900-
1300, 1500-1800.
E.F.TP.WS.B. **[1]**
Fattoria di Basciano*
Viale Duca della Vittoria
159. Tel: 055 8397034. Fax:
055 8399260. *Agriturismo.*
E.F.TP.WS.B. **[2]**
**Fattorie di Galiga e
Vetrice*** Via Trieste 30.
Tel: 055 8397008. Fax: 055
8399041. 0900-1200, 1500-
1700. E.TP.WS.B. **[3]**

WINE MUSEUM
Villa di Poggio Reale,
Rufina. Tel: 055 8396111. B.

VICCHIO
Casa di Giotto (Giotto's
birthplace) Vespignano. Tel:
055 844782. Tue, Thu, Sat,
Sun 1500-1900.

There are seven Chianti denominations. Chianti Classico is the best known, but Chianti Rufina (not to be confused with Ruffino, a producer) has some excellent winemakers.

Rufina is based on the Sieve valley, stretching from Pontassieve, east of Florence, up to Dicomano. The valley is very attractive, but on the whole the towns are not worth visiting. Pontassieve was devastated in World War II, and Rufina has a wine museum in the somewhat dilapidated Villa Poggio Reale, but is choked with traffic. Art lovers may like to visit Giotto's birthplace at Vicchio, near Dicomano.

The geography of the valley is the key to the quality of Chianti Rufina. High vineyards enclosed in a narrow valley that gets very hot in the day and cools rapidly at night yield grapes that make elegant wine with fragrant bouquets and a capacity for long ageing. Chianti Rufina has exactly the same grape composition as the other Chiantis, but if Chianti Classico can be compared to Bordeaux for its rich opulence, Chianti Rufina is more like Burgundy for its elegance.

The wineries – the Right Bank
Starting at the head of the valley, Fattoria di Colognole has a wonderful view right down the valley from the commanding heights where Marchesa Gabriella Spalletti and her sons are re-establishing the family wine business and making some attractive wines.

Further down the valley, the Grati family have two estates, Galiga and Vetrice, which provide a consistent level of quality Chianti Rufina at the lower end of the market. The tower of the Vetrice villa, typically for a Tuscan property, dates back to the 12th century when it was one of a series of defensive towers in the valley. Back over the hills on steep roads up Monte Romito, Madonna delle Grazie al Sasso is an 11th-century church with panoramic views over the valley.

Down the hill from Santa Brigida you come to one of the most beautiful castles in all Tuscany, Castello del Trebbio. Medieval crenellations, thick walls and a Renaissance courtyard combine with a sense of isolation to produce a very special atmosphere. The castle has a place in Medici history: it was here that the Pazzi Conspiracy was hatched in 1478, after which Giuliano de' Medici was murdered in Florence cathedral on Easter day. Technically the estates fall outside the Rufina zone, but the wines are just as good.

There is a short cut involving dirt tracks to the next winery, but probably the easiest route is to go right down to Sieci before cutting back up the hill behind the town to Fattoria dei Bossi. This is one of Rufina's up-and-coming estates. The Vin Santo is superb.

The Left Bank
The other side of the Sieci valley contains the properties of the pioneers of Chianti Rufina. Fattoria di Selvapiana is owned by Francesco Giuntini, who has probably done most for the image of Chianti Rufina abroad with his excellent Riserva Bucerchiale.

Castello di Nipozzano is part of the Frescobaldi empire. This family traces its winemaking back to 1300 AD, and possesses no fewer than 500 hectares of vineyards in Rufina alone. If Chianti Rufina is known at all abroad, it is probably because of the consistent quantity and quality of the Riserva Castello di Nipozzano. Another Frescobaldi fiefdom is Pomino, where Marquess Vittorio degli Albizi planted French grape varieties in the last century.

Frescobaldi's Castello di Nipozzano offers a panoramic view of the Chianti Rufina district.

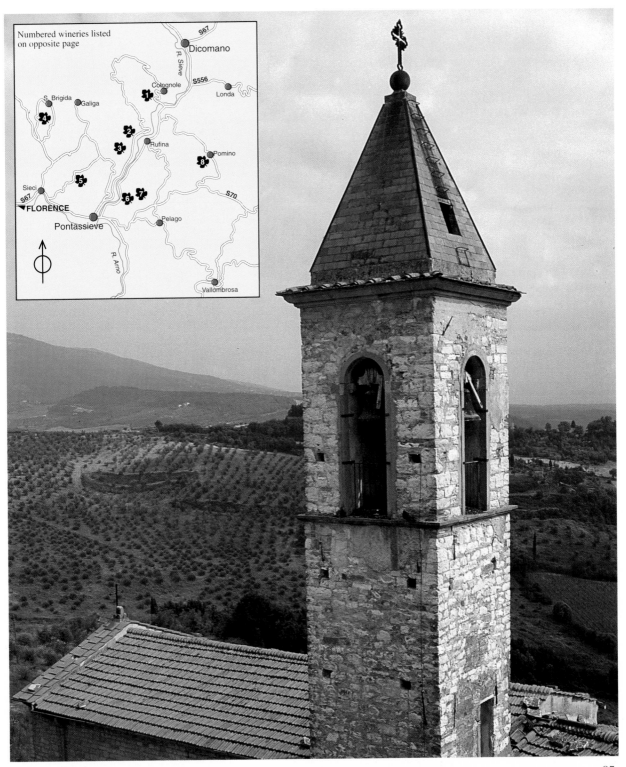

Numbered wineries listed on opposite page

San Gimignano

The first glimpse of San Gimignano's 13 towers is always an exciting moment as you approach the city through the undulating countryside.

Too many visitors, too many gift shops and too much summer heat can be difficult to cope with, but let the coachloads of tourists leave, and it is easy to see why the medieval buildings have become so beloved. The tall towers of the town's feuding families, the narrow streets and courtyards, and the Piazza del Popolo where Dante addressed the Town Council in 1300 (persuading them to change sides in the interminable wars between Siena and Florence) are very romantic.

Vernaccia di San Gimignano

Vernaccia is Tuscany's own original white wine; all the others are based on Trebbiano, except French derivations, such as Pomino, which therefore do not quite count. Vernaccia, however, is literally the 'vernacular' grape variety for the area – it has always been there, and through the centuries it has evolved into something unique. Vernaccia was the first wine to be granted the DOC qualification in 1966 and it has just been made DOCG. But in a wine world enamoured of the big flavours of Chardonnay and spiciness of Sauvignon, its delicacy does not win friends easily.

The problem is that squeaky clean technology combined with high yields in the vineyards renders Vernaccia anonymous and characterless, while a return to the deliberate oxidation of the old-fashioned style in order to find more flavour in the grape is unthinkable.

There are several solutions: dance with the devil and add some Chardonnay to the blend to lift the wine a little; use new-oak *barriques* to add the extra dimension of vanilla and spice; or cut yields drastically and prune hard in the vineyard to get the maximum flavour concentrated in relatively few grapes. Or combine all three solutions.

While the average tourist is happy to buy a souvenir three-bottle pack and not worry overmuch about the quality, there is little incentive for most Vernaccia producers to go to the expense of making a truly fine wine. Nevertheless, there are producers who want to make something world class in San Gimignano and there are good wines to be discovered.

Visiting the producers

In San Gimignano itself there are numerous souvenir shops that also sell wine. Perhaps it is better to concentrate on the towers, the museum and the wonderful Collegiata Church.

If you walk from the town centre down Via San Matteo (incidentally part of the old Pilgrims' Way, the *Via Francigena*, from France to Rome) and just before the town gate turn right into Piazza Sant'Agostino, you will not only have the chance to see some superbly restored frescoes in the church, you will also be able to buy some of San Gimignano's best wines from the Fattoria di Cusona shop in the square. Cusona itself is some way out of town near Poggibonsi and has, incredibly as it may seem, just celebrated 1000 years of recorded winemaking on the estate.

Other producers are closer. Find Montenidoli and Panizzi by locating the *carabinieri* (police) station first – you want the dirt track down the hill by the side of it.

Montenidoli, run by the irrepressible Fagiuoli family, makes consistently high quality Vernaccia in varying styles, including fashionable (and delicious) barrel-fermented. Panizzi is one of San Gimignano's up-and-coming stars.

Other producers of note near to each other include Casale Falchini, who make a particularly successful Riserva Vigna Solatio and a bottle-fermented sparkling Vernaccia; and Teruzzi & Puthod at Fattoria Ponte a Rondolino, who use computer controlled equipment, stainless steel halls and new oak to make Vernaccia that has long been held to be among Italy's finest white wines.

The medieval towers of San Gimignano keep watch over the Vernaccia vineyards.

VAL D'ELSA (cont.)
Tenuta di Scorgiano*
Monteriggioni, 53031
Casole d'Elsa (SI). Tel/Fax:
0577 301020. 0800-2000.
Agriturismo. E.F.G.TF.WS.
(B for groups).

Fattoria Villa Spoiano*
Strada Spoiano 2, 50028
Tavarnelle Val d'Elsa (FI).
Tel/Fax: 055 8077313. (Jan
Karel Waspi). *Agriturismo.*
E.F.G.TP.WS.B.

Chianti Classico

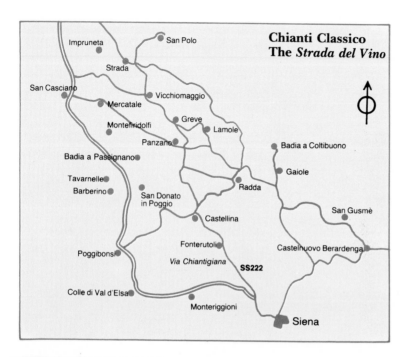

Chianti Classico
The *Strada del Vino*

- Impruneta
- San Polo
- Strada
- San Casciano
- Vicchiomaggio
- Mercatale
- Greve
- Montefiridolfi
- Lamole
- Panzano
- Badia a Coltibuono
- Badia a Passignano
- Gaiole
- Tavarnelle
- Radda
- Barberino
- San Donato in Poggio
- San Gusmè
- Castellina
- Fonterutoli
- Castelnuovo Berardenga
- Poggibonsi
- *Via Chiantigiana* **SS222**
- Colle di Val d'Elsa
- Monteriggioni
- Siena

S CASCIANO
Machiavelli Museum &
Cellars c/o L'Albergaccio,
S Andrea in Percussina (FI).
Tel: 055 828471. Restaurant
hours. Closed Sat am and
Mon. TF.WS.b.

GREVE IN CHIANTI
Az Agr Vecchie Terre di
Montefili Via S Cresci 45,
50022 Greve in Chianti (FI).
Tel: 055 853739. Fax: 055
8544684. Mon-Fri 0800-
1700. E.TP.
Castello di Verrazzano*
Loc Verrazzano, 50022
Greve in Chianti (FI). Tel:
055 854243. Fax: 055
854241. 0900-1700.
E.F.G.TP.WS.B.
Castello Vicchiomaggio*
Via Vicchiomaggio 4, 50022
Greve in Chianti (FI). Tel:
055 854079. Fax: 055
853911. *Agriturismo*,
restaurant. E.F.G.TP.WS.B.
Bottega del Chianti
Classico Via Battisti 4. Tel:
055 853631. WS.

Chianti Classico is the premier Chianti
region. It has always had more stringent
regulations than the other six Chianti
areas, a fact recognized by the award of
its own long-awaited separate DOCG
appellation in 1995, finally confirming
its distance from the other regions.

For a long time, attention has been
focused on the grape mix of Chianti
Classico. The original 19th-century
formula called for white grapes to be
part of the *uvaggio*. This was designed to
produce early-drinking, everyday wines,
and still holds good today. But when
modern producers came to make serious
long-lived wines – the Chianti Riservas
that are the area's fine wines – they
found the white grape rule a handicap.

The solution was to go outside
DOCG regulations and produce what
came to be called Super Tuscan wines.
These could be 100 per cent Sangiovese,
or, conforming to international taste,
they could have an addition of more
than the permitted amount of Cabernet
Sauvignon to give the wine greater body.

Traditionally, Chianti is aged in
large Slavonian oak barrels that last
for years and give very little of their
oakiness (because of size and age) to
the wine. But modern taste,
especially in the export market,
required experiments with the vanilla
oakiness that comes from using new
and almost new French oak *barriques*.

Super Tuscans used to be the
excitement of Chianti – the
combination of *barriques* and
Cabernet was just too seductive, but
now the new DOCG regulations
finally allow the use of 100 per cent
Sangiovese for Chianti Classico, thus
removing one of the major incentives
to declassify an estate's best wine.

Attention has now moved to the
vineyards. What is the ideal density of
vines per hectare? What is the optimum
yield, balancing quality with quantity?
What is the best clone of Sangiovese for
which site? All these questions are being
addressed by the Chianti 2000 Project
overseen by the Consorzio Chianti
Classico growers' association.

Of the Super Tuscans, the more
successful ones, Antinori's Tignanello
or Montevertine's Le Pergole Torte for
example, continue to flourish, and, as
DOC/G regulations are continually
modified, it is likely that they too will
eventually be drawn into the official
classification system.

Chianti Classico touring
Chianti Classico is the most developed
part of Italy for wine tourism. Roadside
kiosks selling an estate's wine are quite
common. Wine shops in the local villages
are used to tourists. The facility to stay on
a wine estate (*agriturismo*) and to book
ahead for meals and snacks with a tasting
is widespread. And, for the really
enthusiastic, it is quite easy to find courses
on Tuscan cooking and wine appreciation

organized by the producers themselves. The quickest way to get anywhere in Chianti Classico is to use the fast road that runs from Florence to Siena and to turn off into Chianti at the most appropriate point. Otherwise, a good flavour of the region can be had by following the old main road, the Via Chiantigiana, through the heart of Chianti Classico. You will need a good map of the area; the Consorzio del Marchio Storico (the Chianti Classico growers' association) has its offices in Sant'Andrea in Percussina, near San Casciano, and publishes the best available.

Start at the Consorzio Chianti Classico's offices. These are in the house that was Machiavelli's refuge while he wrote *The Prince* while an exile from Florence. Just opposite is L'Albergaccio, which has been a *taverna* since Machiavelli's day, and is now a trattoria. The owners of the trattoria are also the custodians of the Machiavelli museum. If the trattoria is open, the museum and cellars are open. If not, *pazienza*.

Enoteca del Chianti Classico Piazzetta Santa Croce 3. Tel: 055 853297. WS.
Enoteca Sant'Anna Via Stecchi 1. Tel: 055 853095. WS.

PANZANO
Fattoria di Montagliari
Via di Montagliari 29, Panzano in Chianti (FI). Tel: 055 852014. Fax: 055 852804. 0900-1200, 1500-1700. Restaurant.
E.G.S.TP.WS.B.

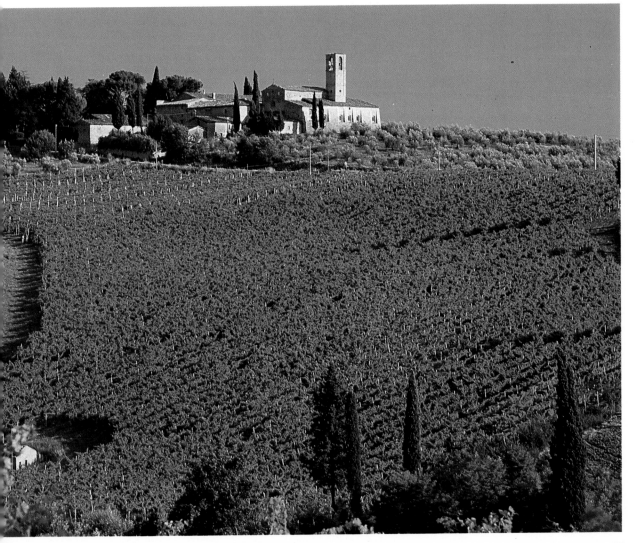

PANZANO (cont.)
Enoteca del Chianti
Classico Via G da Verrazzano
8. Tel: 055 852128. WS.

BARBERINO
Fattoria Casa Sola* Loc
Cortine. Tel: 055 8075028.
Fax: 055 8059194.
Agriturismo. 0930-1200, 1500-
1900. E.F.S.TF.WS.b.
Isole e Olena Loc Isole 1.
Tel: 055 8072763. Fax: 055
8072236. 0900-1200, 1500-
1800. E.F.G.S.TF.WS.B.
Castello di Monsanto*
Via Monsanto 8. Tel: 055
8059000. Fax: 055 8059049.
0800-1230, 1400-1800.
E.F.TP.WS. (B for groups
and guided tastings).
Az Agr Casa Emma*
S Donato in Poggio.Tel: 055
8072859. Fax: 055 667707.
0900-1900. E.TF.WS.

CASTELLINA IN CHIANTI
Poderi Castellare di
Castellina Loc Castellare.
Tel/Fax: 0577 740490.
0900-1200, 1500-1800. E.
(TP for groups). WS.B.
Enoteca Il Cantuccio Via
Ferruccio 25. Tel: 0577
741143. WS.
Bottega del Vino Chianti
Classico Via della Rocca
10. Tel: 0577 740247. WS.

VAGLIAGLI
Fattoria della Aiola Tel:
0577 322615. Fax: 0577
322509. 0900-1300, 1500-
1900. E.F.G.S.TP.WS.B.
Borgo Scopeto 53010. Tel:
0577 356827. Fax: 0577
356736. 0900-1300, 1600-
1800. E.TP.WS.B.

RADDA IN CHIANTI
Podere Capaccia* Loc
Capaccia. Tel/Fax: 0577
738385. 0900-1200, 1400-
1700. E.F.G.TF.WS. (TP, B
for groups).

*The old hamlet of San Felice has been restored by the
wine company and is a working community once more.*

The wine route – Greve

The first town of note along the Via
Chiantigiana is Greve. Piazza Matteotti,
the enormous market place that is the
heart of the town, is an attractive
square with shops under the porticoes
that are well used to the tourist and sell
wild boar sausages, olive oil and Chianti
Classico. The statue is to Giovanni da
Verrazzano, the discoverer of New York
Bay, who came from the nearby castle.

Just before Greve, if you come from
Florence there are several producers'
wine kiosks and a little further on, up
the hill from its own shop, the castle of
Vicchiomaggio. Here Englishman John
Matta and his wife Paola produce a
wide range of Chianti Classico wines
including the superb Vigna Petri, made
from 50-year-old vines cultivated in the
old-fashioned way, that is in clumps
and trained up trees.

Moving on from Greve down the
Via Chiantigiana towards Panzano, the
next stop might be for lunch or a tasting
at Fattoria di Montagliari, where
Giovanni Cappelli makes long-lived Vin
Santo, excellent Chianti and even some
balsamic vinegar. The trattoria attached
to his property has the highest
recommendation, the owner eats there.

Over the other side of the valley can be
glimpsed Villa Vignamaggio, the setting
for the Kenneth Branagh film of *Much
Ado about Nothing* and, reputedly, the
birthplace of the Mona Lisa.

Panzano to San Donato

Up the hill to Panzano, where the old
town has long burst its walls and
sprawled out over the top of the hill.
The castle was destroyed as long ago as
1260, but the event is commemorated
annually every April. The church of
San Leolino, just down the hill towards
Castellina outside the town, has
terracottas by Della Robbia and a
wonderful view over the Pesa valley.
Below you is the Conca of Panzano,
site of some of the most prestigious
Chianti Classico vineyards.

Down the hill from Panzano, cross
the Pesa and take the sharp right up the
other side of the valley to La Piazza (a
good trattoria, Osteria alla Piazza) and
along a winding dirt track to a T-
junction, right to San Donato in
Poggio, a typical medieval *borgo* (village)
with an attractive Romanesque church
on its outskirts, or left towards
Castellina past Casa Emma and
Fattoria La Ripa.

Just outside San Donato is a pair of
contrasting estates. Isole e Olena is one
of the innovators in Chianti Classico;
here Paolo de Marchi makes his
excellent 100 per cent Sangiovese wine
Cepparello and experiments with grape
varieties as diverse as Syrah and
Chardonnay. Further on towards
Poggibonsi on the same dirt track is
Castello di Monsanto, famous for its
long-lived and elegant Chiantis
designed to evolve slowly over the years.

However you arrive at Castellina, it
quickly becomes obvious that this is a
working town in the heart of the wine
industry. Greve is positively trippery

compared to Castellina. Have lunch at Trattoria La Torre and watch it fill up with vineyard workers and winery employees sure of getting good food.

Vineyards surround the ruins of the Monastery of San Niccolo just outside the town towards Poggibonsi, where the Castellare estate makes organic wines.

From Castellina the Via Chiantigiana goes south to Fonterutoli, where the Mazzei family make top-class Chiantis. Strike out over the hills to Vagliagli to visit wineries such as Fattoria della Aiola and cut back up to Radda, one of the major centres of Chianti. Dirt tracks are the norm in this area, but do not be alarmed, there is always a stretch of asphalt further on, and the dust and gravel give any trip the status of an adventure.

Radda

Radda itself is sleepy. The Palazzo del Podestà, with the coats of arms that adorn it, is evocative of medieval times when this was the capital of the *Lega del Chianti* defensive alliance of Radda, Gaiole and Castellina, but one gets the feeling that the last time it was sacked, in 1478, the town expired. There is, however, one good place to stay, the Relais Fattoria Vignale, which

Castello di Brolio is the home of the illustrious Ricasoli family.

RADDA IN CHIANTI (cont.)
Fattoria di Montevertine*
Loc Montevertine. Tel: 0577 738009. Fax: 0577 738265. Mon-Fri 0900-1200, 1400-1700. E.F.G.TP.WS.b.
Podere Pruneto* Loc Pruneto. Tel/Fax: 0577 738013. 0900-1100, 1500-1700. E.F.TF.WS.b.
Podere Terreno* alla Via di Volpaia. Tel/Fax: 0577 738312. *Agriturismo*. 1000-1300, 1500-1800. E.F.G.TP.WS.B.

RADDA IN CHIANTI (cont.)
Enoteca Vignale Fattoria Vignale, Via Pianigiani 9. Tel: 0577 738012. Fax: 0577 738730. 0900-1300, 1500-2000. Closed Jan-mid March. Hotel. E.F.TF.WS.
Fattoria Castello di Volpaia* Loc Volpaia, 53017. Tel: 0577 738066. Fax: 0577 738619. 0900-1230, 1500-1930. Olive oil mill. E.F.TP.WS.B.

GAIOLE IN CHIANTI
Badia a Coltibuono Loc Badia a Coltibuono. Tel: 0577 749498. Fax: 0577 749235. Sat 1100-1300. Closed Aug, Nov-Mar. Abbey. E.F.WS at estate shop.
Barone Ricasoli* Cantine del Castello di Brolio. Tel: 0577 749066. Fax: 0577 749070. Mon-Sat 0900-1200, 1300-1900. Sun, hols 1100-1900. E.TF.WS.B.
Riecine Loc Riecine. Tel/Fax: 0577 749098. 0800-1700. E.G.TF.WS.b.
Castello di San Polo in Rosso Tel: 0577 746045. Fax: 0577 746153. 0800-1200, 1300-1700. E.F.G.TP.WS.B.
Fattoria Vistarenni srl* Loc Vistarenni. Tel: 0577 738186. Fax: 0577 738476. 0900-1300, 1500-1700. F.TP.WS.B.
Enoteca Montagnani Via Bandinelli 9. Tel: 0577 749517.

SAN GUSMÉ
Agricola San Felice* Loc S Felice. Tel: 0577 359087. Fax: 0577 359223. Mon-Thu 0830-1630. E.F.TP.WS.B.

AREZZO
Fattoria Villa La Selva* Montebenichi, Bucine (AR). Tel: 0574 720787. Fax: 0574 650640. 0900-1200, 1500-1900. E.F.TF.WS.b.

combines hotel, wine shop and winery on one site.

The excitement around Radda comes from its wine producers. On one side there is Fattoria di Montevertine, Sergio Manetti's great challenge to the received wisdom of Chianti Classico. The estate opted out of the Consorzio Chianti Classico early in its life, when Manetti found that if he belonged to it he was legally obliged to make wine in a way he knew was madness. He knew he should concentrate on the Sangiovese grape and have nothing to do with white grape blends in Chianti for the type of long-lived wines he was aiming at. Time has proved Manetti right and his early bid for independence years before other producers followed his example with other Super Tuscan alternatives to Chianti has made his name.

Another great character of Tuscan winemaking has the estate just up the hill from Montevertine, Podere Capaccia. Giampaolo Pacini is a businessman from Prato, but he was also trained as an enologist. His story is typical of many in Chianti Classico. Seeking the good life in the country he came to Chianti in the 1970s, when many of the smaller hamlets were falling to rack and ruin. He found Capaccia, an abandoned group of houses, decaying after the families who originally lived there left and went to the towns to find more lucrative work.

Slowly, Pacini has rebuilt the main house of the complex and shelters his winery in other partially rebuilt houses. He has also developed gastronomic tourism to its ultimate stage, offering fascinating courses in recreating historical Tuscan cooking, and doing the research himself.

Over the other side of the valley is another medieval complex on a grander scale. This is Castello di Volpaia. The story is familiar; Carlo and Giovanella Stianti come from Milan and have spent decades restoring much of the village in a hilltop site. One house is for the fermentation tanks, one house contains the ageing cellars, one is the offices, another is the olive oil press, yet another is the vinegar plant. Much of the village is in fact a carefully hidden winery. And the church is used for an annual art exhibition of the highest standing.

Gaiole

Just down the hill from Volpaia is Podere Terreno, which provides bed, breakfast, dinner and its own wine.

From Radda, take the road east to Badia a Coltibuono, perhaps via Vistarenni in the commune of Gaiole just to taste the wines and admire the impressive Venetian-style villa.

Coltibuono is one of Chianti Classico's great estates and, hidden in the woods on the site of a former monastery, it is in a very tranquil setting. Lorenza de' Medici, wife of the owner and author of many books on Italian cooking, runs courses on Tuscan cuisine here. Naturally, there is a trattoria as part of the complex.

Here, you pick up signs to the *Strada dei Castelli del Chianti*, which makes for less of a wine-intensive tour, but nevertheless leads to properties such as Castello di San Polo in Rosso, which is frescoed church, castle and wine estate rolled into one.

At Coltibuono, stay in Chianti Classico and go on to the castles, or take the road over the hills to Chianti Aretino to visit the more out of the way estates, such as Villa La Selva, whose owner, industrialist Sergio Carpini, is determined to make a showplace for wine.

The next castle is Brolio, back in the commune of Gaiole. This wonderful neo-Gothic pile was built in the last century on the ruins of a more ancient castle by the man who was Italy's second Prime Minister and formulator of the Chianti *cépage*, Baron Bettino Ricasoli. The family have recently taken back control of the estate after a period of sad decline in the hands of a multinational company and the latest vintages are markedly better.

From Brolio it is a short distance to San Felice, which is a sensitively restored medieval village now combining hotel, restaurant and, at 190 hectares, one of Tuscany's biggest wineries. On a clear day you can see the towers of San Gimignano in the far distance in a landscape that cannot have changed much in hundreds of years. It is a magical sight.

SIENA
Enoteca Italiana Fortezza Medicea, 53100 Siena Tel: 0577 288497. Fax: 0577 270717. Every day 1200-1300. TP.WS.

Siena's Enoteca Permanente (left) is sited in the east bastion of the great Medici fortress. The wide munitions staircase leads to the vaults where over 600 Italian wines are displayed, selected by a tasting panel. The list is not comprehensive, but it does genuinely include some of the best wines in Italy. Three are opened every day for tasting, but any wine is available by the glass for a very modest sum.

The huge medieval cathedral (below) is another attraction.

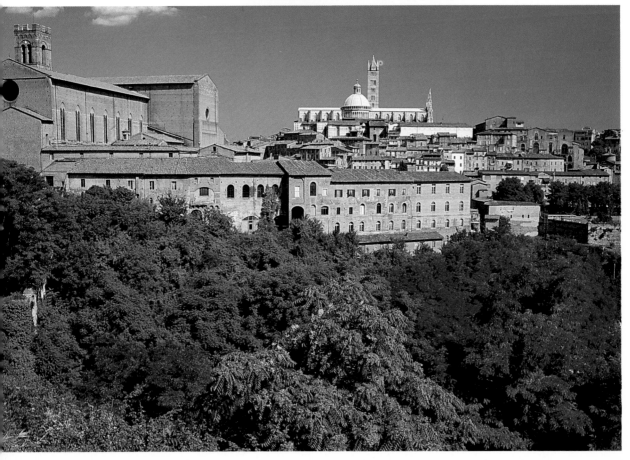

Montalcino

South of Siena the countryside changes dramatically. The hills of Chianti with their olive trees, vines and woods give way to the hills of Le Crete Senesi, a beautiful area to travel through, especially before the harvest when the cornfields and sunflowers gild the hills with different shades of yellow, giving the few clumps of cypresses in their midst an almost surreal air.

The SS2 from Siena is part of the old Pilgrims Way to Rome, the Via Francigena, that also runs through the centre of San Gimignano.

Buonconvento is the first town of note along the route. Its 14th-century walls are still in good repair. A yellow tourist sign signals the turning to the Abbey of Monte Oliveto Maggiore, where the site and its frescoes make the detour worthwhile.

The town of Montalcino

Perhaps only Alba, in Piedmont, has such an intense atmosphere of wine as Montalcino. There is a certain mystique about the fabled wine that brings an otherwise sleepy town alive.

There are several wine shops in Montalcino, but the one essential stop for a restorative glass of wine and perhaps a taste of local salami or pecorino cheese is the combined Enoteca and wine bar in the castle.

This was the last fortress of the Sienese Republic to hold out against combined Imperial and Florentine forces from 1555 until 1559. The event is recorded by a plaque on the castle walls which talks of the 'Medici Robbers', and even now the Florentines are spoken of with little fondness.

The great Brunello

The credit for the invention of Brunello goes to the ancestor of its most famous producers, the Biondi Santi family.

It was Clemente Santi who created Brunello in the 1850s when the potential of the Brunello clone of the Sangiovese grape was identified. Franco Biondi Santi and his son Jacopo continue the tradition today. Their wines are famously long lived and famously expensive too.

Brunello has undergone several changes of style since it was first created and along the way has acquired the reputation of being a wine that takes years to come to its peak. However, with the exception of Biondi Santi wines, this is largely a myth. Five to ten years after the vintage is enough.

By law the wine must age in barrel for at least three and a half years, and then in bottle for six months to make up a four year total. This is fine with a good vintage. But what happens with a bad vintage? This is a long time in barrel for modern wines. Surely without the finest grapes the wine will not have sufficient structure to survive the lengthy ageing process?

This is why Rosso di Montalcino was created as a DOC wine in 1984. Rosso is made of the Brunello grape too, but it only needs one year's ageing, thereby allowing producers to select the second grade grapes for Rosso in good years and dedicate all the grapes to Rosso in bad years. The public love it, too. Rosso di Montalcino is a simpler and fruitier version of Brunello with a bit of structure nevertheless and some of the cachet of its more illustrious cousin.

The other wine of the area is Moscadello, a traditional sweet wine based on a variant of the Moscato grape.

Visiting the estates

Montalcino's vineyard area can roughly be divided into three sub-zones that produce wines of broadly differing characteristics, although, of course,

CASTELNUOVO DELL' ABATE
Tenuta di Collosorbo Loc Villa A Sesta 25. Tel/Fax: 0577 835534. 0900-1200, 1500-2000. TP.WS.B.

MONTALCINO
Altesino* Loc Altesino. Tel: 0577 806208. Fax: 0577 806131. 0900-1900. E.G. Danish TP.WS.b.
Fattoria dei Barbi* Tel: 0577 848277. Fax: 0577 849356. Mon-Fri 0900-1300, 1500-1800. Sat, Sun 1430-1730. E.F.G.TF.WS.b.
Banfi* Castello di Poggio alle Mura. Tel: 0577 840111. Fax: 0577 840205. Glass museum in castle every day1000-1930. Cellars Mon-Fri office hours. E.F.G.TP.WS.B.
Tenuta Caparzo* Loc Caparzo. Tel: 0577 848390. Fax: 0577 849377. 1000-1200, 1500-1700. E.F.G.TF.WS.B.
Az Agr Case Basse c/o Via dei Frassini 39, 20156 Milano. Tel: 02 461544. Fax: 02 48195341). TF.B.
Az Agr Siro Pacenti Loc Pelagrilli. Tel/Fax: 0577 848622. 0800-1200, 1400-1800. E.F.TF.B.
Fattoria Poggio Antico Loc Poggio Antico. Tel/Fax: 0577 848044. 0900-2000. E.F.TP.WS.B.
Tenuta Valdicava* Loc Valdicava. Tel: 0577 848261. Fax: 0577 848008. E.TF.B.

S ANGELO IN COLLE
Tenuta Col d'Orcia* Tel: 0577 808001. Fax: 0577 864018. 0900-1230, 1430-1800. E.F.G.TF.WS.B.
Az Agr Talenti Loc Piandiconte. Tel/Fax: 0577 864043. 0800-1300, 1500-1800. TF.WS.B.

such generalizations are easily refuted by an individual winemaker's style.

In general, then, the wines from the north of Montalcino are less full-bodied but more elegant. Wines from the east are bigger, fuller wines as their vineyards are sheltered from any bad weather. Those to the south reflect the warmer weather and are the biggest, most powerful wines of all.

Whatever wineries you visit Brunello provides a consistently high quality wine. Highlights include: Fattoria dei Barbi, which makes its own cheese and salami as well as having its own trattoria; Poggio Antico, which has its own restaurant and makes top quality modern Brunellos; Case Basse – a cult wine in Italy; Talenti – one of the magical winemakers of the older generation; and Col d'Orcia, one of the most widely available good quality wines. Banfi is the biggest producer; American owned, it provides a wide range of wines in very approachable styles.

Don't miss the Abbey of Sant' Antimo outside Castelnuovo dell'Abate just south of Montalcino, reputedly founded by Charlemagne and restored to magnificence only this century. The new community of monks are famous for Gregorian chant.

The logo of the Consorzio of Brunello (above) bears the symbol of Montalcino, the leaves of the holm oak. The countryside around Montalcino (below) is wooded and hilly, with sunflowers in the valley and vineyards on the hillsides.

Montepulciano

The heraldic griffin – the symbol on the logo of the Consorzio of Vino Nobile producers (above) – gives its name to Grifi wine (right).

ACQUAVIVA DI MONTEPULCIANO
Poderi Boscarelli Via di Montenero 28, Loc Cervognano. Tel/Fax: 0577 767277. (Paola or Luca De Ferrari). 0900-1700. E.F.TF.WS.B.
Tenuta Vallocaia Terre Bindella, Via delle Tre Berte 10/a. Tel: 0578 767777. Fax: 0578 767255. (Tiziana Calvin). 0830-1700. G.TP.WS.B.

MONTEPULCIANO
Avignonesi* Via Gracciano del Corso. Tel: 0578 757872. Fax: 0578 757847. (Gaia Anderson). E.F.TP.B.
Cantina del Redi* Via di Colazzi 5. Tel: 0578 757166. Fax: 0578 716051.Mon-Fri 1000-1300, 1500-1900. Sun 1000-1900. E.TP.B.
Fattoria Le Casalte* Via del Termine 2, Loc S Albino. Tel: 0578 799138. Fax: 06 9306988. (Paola Silvestri Barioffi, Chiara Barioffi). 0900-1800. E.TF.WS.b.
Az Agr Contucci* Via del Teatro 1. Tel/Fax: 0578 757006. (Alamanno Contucci, Adamo Pallecchi). 0900-1230, 1430-1830. E.F.TF.WS. (B for groups).

About half an hour's drive east from Montalcino is its great rival, Montepulciano, the zone of the splendidly named Vino Nobile di Montepulciano.

Papal Pienza
Pienza is on the way. There is a wine excuse to stop here (a good Enoteca). However, the birthplace of Aeneas Silvio Piccolomini, Pope Pius II, largely rebuilt by him in a felicitous time for architecture (1459-1464), should also be visited for its architectural splendour. In gastronomic terms the town is known for its cheeses, pecorino di Pienza and ricotta.

Vino Nobile di Montepulciano
The first wine in Italy to be granted the top ranking DOCG status was Vino Nobile di Montepulciano. Exactly why it is called Vino Nobile is uncertain. The wine has always been known for its quality, since at least the 17th century, but more likely the epithet *nobile* refers to the fact that this was the wine produced on the estates of the noble occupants of the grand houses in Montepulciano. Compared with Brunello, it has the advantage of being a more approachable wine ready to drink sooner because of its fewer years of barrel ageing.

Vino Nobile is very similar in make-up to Chianti. The major grape is Sangiovese, here called Prugnolo

because of its supposed plum-like taste, together with small percentages of Canaiolo, Mammolo, Malvasia and Trebbiano. So, just like Chianti, it varies in style, although, unlike Chianti, it is of a consistently high quality.

Some producers make Vino Nobile with an almost New World richness, full of tight fruit and tannin. Others make a wine of soft aromatic elegance.

Like Brunello, Vino Nobile also has a younger second wine version, Rosso di Montepulciano. This ensures that only the best grapes go into Vino Nobile, but there is no agreement at all about what style the Rosso should have; young and fruity like a Beaujolais Nouveau, or traditionally structured like an everyday Chianti? In any case, only small quantities are produced.

The other wines of the area are Chianti Colli Senesi and Bianco Vergine Valdichiana – honest local wines.

Montepulciano
The hill town of Montepulciano is about 14km (9 miles) from Pienza. The first feature you see is Sangallo's Renaissance masterpiece, the church of San Biagio, halfway up the slope.

The whole town is something of an architect's dream; it is full of Renaissance palaces from the early 16th century, built for the nobles whose estates provided the Vino Nobile.

Park outside the town at Porta al Prato and begin the climb up the main street, Via Gracciano del Corso. The wine shops begin almost at once. But just at the corner, opposite the stone lion on a pillar, the *Marzocco* that records the town's medieval allegiance to Florence, is the lovely Palazzo Avignonesi, another masterpiece from Sangallo.

Avignonesi is one of the area's top producers. You can taste the Vino Nobile, the Grifi (Sangiovese and

Cabernet), the Merlot, the Marzocco (Chardonnay) and Tuscany's best (and most expensive) Vin Santo in the *palazzo*.

Climbing further up into the town there is a constant succession of delightful buildings, reaching a climax with the stunningly operatic Piazza Grande. The Town Hall, the Palazzo Comunale, is a miniature version of Florence's Palazzo Vecchio, and the cathedral and *palazzi* that form the other three sides of the square are like something out of a stage set; they are a perfectly designed ensemble.

Several of the *palazzi* have ancient cellars dug into the hill of the town.

Cantina del Redi is one of the most interesting. Don't miss Palazzo Contucci on the edge of Piazza Grande; this is another good wine excuse, for Alamanno Contucci is President of the Vino Nobile Consorzio, and a noted producer himself.

Outside the town of Montepulciano itself the Vino Nobile zone extends over the surrounding hills. There is an interruption for the Val di Chiana (Vino Nobile regulations stipulate a minimum vineyard altitude of 250m/ 820ft) to the east and then an island of Vino Nobile the other side of the valley around the hilltop town of Valiano.

MONTEPULCIANO (cont.)
Fattoria di Gracciano, Via Umbria 63, Loc Montepulciano Stazione. Tel: 0578 708228. Fax: 0578 707097. (Giancarlo Vota, Gino Collini). 0900-1200, 1400-1700. Sat 0900-1200. E.F.T.P.WS. (B for groups).

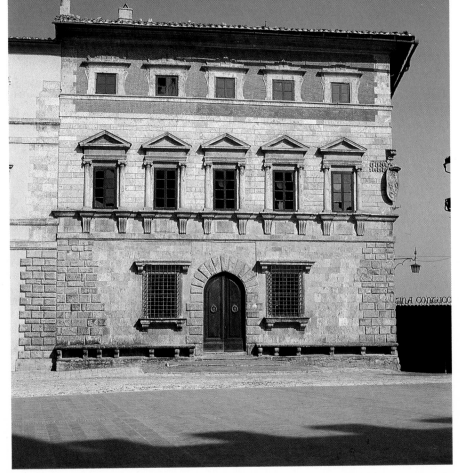

Palazzo Contucci is one of Montepulciano's many beautiful buildings, a classic example of the Renaissance town palace of a noble family.

Food of Tuscany

FOR FURTHER INFORMATION

Movimento del Turismo del Vino (Toscana) c/o Podere Capaccia, 53017 Radda in Chianti (SI). Tel: 0574 582426. Fax: 0574 582428. List of all Tuscan members of Movement for Wine Tourism.

Consorzio Vino Chianti Lungarno Corsini 4, 50123 Firenze. Tel: 055 212333. Fax: 055 210271. Chianti Rufina Wine Roads pamphlet.

Consorzio Marchio Storico del Chianti Classico Via Scopeti 155, S Andrea in Percussina, 50026 S Casciano (FI). Tel: 055 8228245. Fax: 055 8228173. Essential Chianti Classico map.

Consorzio Brunello di Montalcino Costa del Municipio 1, Montalcino (SI). Tel: 0577 848246. Fax: 055 849425.

Consorzio Morellino di Scansano Via XX Settembre 49c, 58054 Scansano (GR). Tel/Fax: 0564 507710.

Consorzio San Gimignano Via della Rocca 1, 53037 San Gimignano (SI). Tel: 0577 940108. Fax: 0577 942088.

Consorzio Vino Nobile di Montepulciano Via delle Case Nuove 15, 53045 Montepulciano (SI). Tel: 0578 757812. Fax: 0578 758213.

Azienda Promozione Turistica Firenze Via A Manzoni 16, 50121 Firenze. Tel: 055 23320. Fax: 055 2346284. Numerous booklets about area around Florence.

Azienda Promozione Turistica Livorno Piazza Civica 4, 57123 Livorno. Tel: 0586 822111 Fax: 0586 884057. Very useful booklet on Livorno coast *La Strada del Vino* (also in English).

Agriturismo – staying on a wine estate

In the main wine-producing areas of Italy there is now a growing demand for self-catering houses and apartments for rent, especially during the summer.

Tuscany is particularly rich in this type of accommodation. Wine producers have converted their villa stable blocks or outlying barns into holiday homes, and some have even converted their own castles or *Fattorie* into hotels.

Such accommodation is very popular, but there is no standardization of facilities at all: some are hotel standard, others are frankly depressing.

Many of the estates recommended for their wine in the information panels of this book also offer *agriturismo*. Ask for further details in order to check on exactly the type of accommodation offered, or, if in doubt, book through a reputable travel agent.

FOOD SPECIALITIES

Until the quality of the ingredients is appreciated, Tuscan food can seem severe and parsimonious. This is, perhaps, the reason for the fame of *Bistecca alla fiorentina*, a generous rib steak, an island in the sea of soups and beans.

But as good members of this nation of food critics, the Tuscans are fascinated by their food, and their preoccupation is above all with the quality of the raw ingredients.

When the wine estate of Castello della Sala was officially opened to the world's press a few years ago, what really excited the prestigious Antinori company was that they could serve a meal composed of meat, fruit, vegetables and wine, with all the products coming from their own estate. There were no problems about hiring internationally renowned chefs; the food consisted of the freshest ingredients, simply cooked. Typically Tuscan.

Olive oil

Tuscany is justly famous for its simple foods. The extra-vergine olive oil is so fruity, rich and thick, it is almost a meal in itself. But it is neither as plentiful or as cheap now as it was before the great frost of 1985 which destroyed so many of Chianti's abundant olive trees. New shoots have now sprung from many of the frost-blasted trees, but it may still be some years before olive oil production recovers fully.

Olive oil is used for cooking, but its main purpose is to bring out the flavour of cooked foods. The *Bistecca* and the *Ribollita*, bean soup that is cooked twice, 'reboiled', is delicious laced with local olive oil.

Liver is much loved in Tuscany. A favourite dish is *Fegatelli* (or *Fegatini di maiale all'uccelletto*), a type of kebab of pig's liver, bay leaf, and traditional Tuscan unsalted bread. *Crostini di fegatini* is a dish of toasted rounds of Tuscan bread served with a delicious liver and anchovy paste.

Game and fish

Pasta is not a traditional Tuscan food, but it does appear in dishes which combine the hunter's catch with rich sauces: *Pappardelle alla lepre*, for example, is wide pasta strips with a hare sauce.

Hunting, once common in the great forests of Tuscany, is still a favourite activity, and it can produce wild boar in various remote parts of Tuscany. But it is more likely to entail the shooting of *conigli* – rabbits, or *uccelletti* – small birds, which are cooked on a spit and eaten bones and all.

The Tuscan coast provides several fish specialities: *Triglie alla livornese* is red mullet cooked with tomatoes, garlic and ginger. *Cèe* or *Cieche alla pisana* are eel fry cooked with olive oil, garlic and sage and served with parmesan. Salt cod, *Baccalà*, is a speciality of Livorno, and is cooked with tomatoes and potatoes.

Finocchio – fennel, is baked with butter and parmesan as an accompaniment to roast meats, and is used to great effect to flavour a special type of salami, the *finocchiona*.

FESTIVALS

April: FLORENCE: Easter festival, the 'Explosion of the Cart' with fireworks.
May: PONTASSIEVE: *Toscanello d'Oro*, an exhibition of Chianti wine.
July, August: SIENA: the Palio, the most famous city horse race in Italy.
August, last Sunday: MONTEPULCIANO: *Bravio delle Botti*, a costume parade followed by wine-barrel race.
September, second half: LUCCA: *Mostra dei Prodotti Tipici*, wine, oil and honey.
September: GREVE IN CHIANTI: *Mostra Mercato del Vino Chianti Classico*, the high point of the Chianti-showing calendar.
September: AREZZO: Joust of the Saracen, a costume tournament.

THE GALLO NERO (BLACK COCKEREL)
This emblem of the *Chianti Classico Consorzio*, a familiar neck label on their members' bottles, was the symbol of the medieval Chianti League.

It recalls the meeting of two knights who were to have ridden out from Siena and Florence exactly at cockcrow, towards each other, along the Via Chiantigiana. Their meeting point was supposed to establish the future boundary between the warring cities.

The black cockerel of Florence, scrawny and underfed, woke his rider up much earlier than the pampered Sienese cockerel. And consequently the riders met at Fonterutoli, much nearer Siena than Florence.

TRAVEL AGENT
Noble Wine Trails
Piazza Grande 11, 57123 Livorno. Tel: 0586 895243. Fax: 0586 884694. Specializes in arranging 'made-to-measure' wine tours of Tuscany for individuals and groups.

The central café and wine shop in Montalcino retains its title of fiaschetteria *from the days when wine was sold in straw-covered flasks* (fiaschi).

Central Italy

The tourist brochures and guidebooks are full of the phrase *L'Italia ha un cuore verde* (Italy has a green heart), but it is true nevertheless that Umbria as a region is a gentle, green and pleasant land, with enchanting landscapes of green hills and dense forests, and some of the country's most beautiful towns. The smokestacks of industry are confined to the city of Terni. With this exception, Umbria is a jewel of the Middle Ages: Gubbio is the archetypal medieval town; Perugia is a magnificent fortress on a hill; Orvieto's cathedral is one of the wonders of Italy; Spoleto is more cosmopolitan but just as antique. Assisi needs no comment, except perhaps that even if St Francis had not inspired its immense basilica it would still be worth visiting for its hillside setting. Both historically and vinously there is an overlap with the Lazio region, where the cities of Bolsena and Viterbo share an Etruscan heritage with Umbria.

For wine lovers there are three areas of interest in Central Italy: Orvieto, Torgiano, and Montefalco.

Everyone has heard of Orvieto, famous for its wine and artistic treasures. Indeed Orvieto wine labels are often distinguished by a picture of the façade of Orvieto's cathedral.

Castello della Sala (see page 105) has been restored by Antinori, whose estates produce some of Central Italy's finest wines.

This wine became popular because of proximity to Tuscany – Chianti producers sold it as their white wine.

Orvieto production extends into the northern tip of Lazio. Around Lake Bolsena they make a white wine with a curious history, and a still more curious name: Est!Est!!Est!!! (see page 105).

Torgiano and Montefalco

South of Perugia, near the famous majolica-producing town of Deruta, is Torgiano. Here the Lungarotti family have established an Italian institution – the Lungarotti winery, with a hotel and an internationally renowned museum of wine-related artefacts.

Just outside Foligno is the town of Montefalco, whose red wines are attracting much interest. Unique to the area is the Sagrantino grape, used to supplement the more usual Sangiovese in Rosso di Montefalco, but also vinified as a red wine in its own right. The taste has been described as reminiscent of blackberries. There is also a *passito* version made with semi-dried grapes.

PRINCIPAL VINEYARD AREAS

Est! Est!! Est!!!

Orvieto Classico

Orvieto

Montefalco

Torgiano

Sansepolcro

Città di Castello

Cortona

Gúbbio

L. Trasimene

Perugia

SS3

Panicale

Città della Pieve

Torgiano

Assisi

SS2

Spello

SS71

Bevagna

Montefalco

Foligno

Bolsena

Orvieto

Todi

L. Bolsena

SS1

Montefiascone

SS3

Tuscania

A1

R. Tiber

Spoleto

Viterbo

Nórcia

Orte

Terni

L. di Vico

Civitavécchia

Civita Castellana

A12

SS2

SS3

Orvieto Country

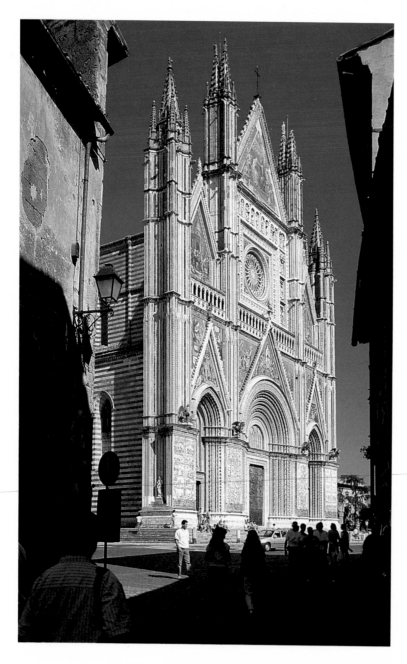

The façade of the cathedral in Orvieto reflects the Italian sunshine like a gilded wedding cake. Inside there is an elaborate series of frescoes. Outside, shops in the cathedral square sell Orvieto's famous white wines.

Perugino; see his *Adoration of the Magi* in S. Maria dei Bianchi.

Orvieto

The sheer rock face on which Orvieto is built makes it a superb defensive site; it was much favoured by the Popes and remained part of the Papal States until 1860. The old town remains largely intact and unspoilt on its table-top position.

The cathedral is unique and though the mosaics on the façade were heavily restored in the 19th century, they follow the original design of the 14th century.

Orvieto wine

Wine-making in Orvieto goes back at least as far as the Etruscans and may even be reflected in the town's name.

One legend has barbarian invaders foiled in their attempt to carry off chalices by the gold metal inexplicably turning to liquid. '*Aurum vetitum,*' they shrieked, giving the city its name, and ran away.

Another story, no doubt put about by wine-makers in the not too distant past, suggests that the *aurum vetitum* was none other than the golden wine that also bears the name Orvieto. It is nonetheless true that the wine, especially the sweeter *abboccato* Orvieto, does have a genuinely golden colour.

Orvieto is a wine waiting to be re-invented. Twenty years ago it was the Chianti producers' white wine for the export market, made in a dry *secco* version or, more often, a medium dry *abboccato* version. Now the *secco* is the predominant style, but modern fermentation techniques and commercial necessity often turn it into yet another crisp, light, white with no particular character at all.

The easiest route to Orvieto from Tuscany is the A1 motorway, the *Autostrada del Sole*.

Various diversions are possible, notably to Chiusi for its National Etruscan Museum and to Città della Pieve, the birthplace of the artist

A view over Lake Bolsena from Grotte di Castro reveals the land of Est!Est!!Est!!!

ALLERONA
Dott. Antonino Scambia Tenuta Antica Selva di Meana* Loc Poggio Barile Tel: 0763 67157. Fax: 0763 67285. (Siria Scambia). 0830-1300, 1500-1800. E.F.TF.WS.B.

CORBARA
Az Agr Decugnano dei Barbi* Loc Fossatello di Corbara, Orvieto. Tel: 0763 308255. Fax: 0763 308118. (Roberta Costantini). 0800-1200, 1400-1800. Cellars of Etruscan origin. TF (TP for groups). WS.B.
Barberani Az Agr Vallesanta* Loc Cereto, Lago di Corbara, Baschi. Tel: 0763 341820. Fax: 0763 340773. (Dott. Luigi Antonio Barberani). 0800-1300, 1400-1700. E.F.TF.WS.

FICULLE
Castello della Sala* Loc La Sala. Tel: 0763 86051. Fax: 0763 86491. (Carla Guarnieri, Annalisa Mancini). TF.WS.B.

ORVIETO SCALO
Villa Pagliano* Loc Castellunchio, 67. Tel/Fax: 0763 304051. (Monica or Ernesto Cotti). Open all year, 0900-1200, 1500-1800. Etruscan tomb at gate of villa. E.TF.WS.B.

The most exciting development recently has been the discovery that Orvieto can be highly successful as a dessert wine, made with grapes affected by noble rot, just like Sauternes. *Muffa nobile*, or noble rot, occurs in the Orvieto region around Lake Corbara where the autumn mists lead to the creation of the *Botrytis cinerea* fungus on the grapes and a consequent shrivelling and concentration of sugars.

Wines such as Antinori's Muffato della Sala, Decugnano dei Barbi's Pourriture Noble and Barberani's Calcaia are proving how successful these luscious dessert wines can be, even if they can only ever be produced in tiny quantities.

Just as interesting is the discovery by Antinori at Castello della Sala that the international grape variety Chardonnay and the local Grechetto can be combined to make a world-class wine, Cervaro della Sala. This is not DOC Orvieto, but it does prove the potential of this part of Umbria.

EST! EST!! EST!!!

The other wine of note in this area lies in the zone of Montefiascone, between Bolsena and Viterbo. Est! Est!! Est!!! can be pleasant enough, but it is normally of only passing interest. The fascination lies in the origin of its Latin name with its plethora of exclamation marks.

The story behind the wine dates back a thousand years. It is said that a certain German prelate, Bishop Fugger, was journeying south to Rome around the year 1000AD, accompanied by a servant whose task it was to travel ahead of his master to find the best inns with the best wine. Having found a suitable hostelry, the servant would write *Est!* on the door to indicate its suitability, and then hurry on to the next place.

On reaching Montefiascone, the servant was so struck by the quality of the local wine that he wrote not one *Est!* but three on the door, complete with exclamation marks. Apparently his master was equally convinced of the quality of the wine, for he died of drinking too much of it, and was buried in the same place. Until the 17th century, a barrel of wine was emptied on the bishop's grave every anniversary of his death.

Perugia and Montefalco

BEVAGNA
Az Agr Adanti* Vocabolo
Arquata. Tel: 0742 360295.
Fax: 0742 361013. (Alvaro
Palini, Daniela Adanti,
Desiderio Bini). 0830-1230,
1430-1800. E.F.TF.WS.B.

MONTEFALCO
**Az Agr Antonelli San
Marco*** Loc S Marco 59.
Tel/Fax: 0742 379158.
(Lamberto Spacchetti). All
year 0900-1200, 1500-1800.
Agriturismo. E.TF.WS.B.
**Val di Maggio A.
Caprai*** Loc Torre. Tel:
0742 378802. Fax: 0742
378422. (Marco Caprai).
0830-1300, 1500-1830.
E.TP.WS.B.
Rocca di Fabbri* Fabbri
di Montefalco. Tel: 0742
399379. Fax: 0742 399199.
(Simona Vitali). 0830-1230,
1400-1830. Closed Jan.
E.F.TF.WS.B.

PERUGIA
**Enoteca Provinciale di
Perugia** Via Ulisse Rocchi
18. Tel: 075 5724824. Tue-
Sat 1000-1330, 1600-2130,
Sun 1000-1300. Closed
Mon. TP.WS.

Umbria, the green heart of Italy, is a
fertile region; but wine has never been a
major component of its agriculture.
The grape accounts for less than five
per cent of its produce: precedence is
given to livestock, cereals, and tobacco.

There are two approaches to
northern Umbria and the region's
capital of Perugia. One way is via Città
di Castello and the Tiber Valley; the
DOC red and white wine Colli
Altotiberini comes from here but is of
mainly local interest.

The other way is via Cortona and
Lake Trasimene. DOC Colli del
Trasimeno is mainly of local interest
too. More interesting is to reflect, as
you pass them by, on the village names,
Ossaia (ossuary) and Sanguineto
(bloody), which indicate the area of
Hannibal's victory in 217 BC, at the
battle of Lake Trasimene.

Perugia
Perugia is a great cultural centre and
combines the rural simplicity of
Umbria with the style of a university
city. Raphael began his career in
Perugia, and the painters Pinturicchio
and Perugino also worked here. The

Galleria Nazionale dell'Umbria, one of
Italy's finest art galleries, is housed in
the magnificent Palazzo dei Priori.
Don't miss the Archeological Museum
and the Etruscan Tomb of the
Volumnii just outside the town to the
south. For an overview, and tasting, of
Umbrian wines, visit the Enoteca
Provinciale di Perugia.

Torgiano
A short distance to the south lies
Torgiano, where the world's wine press
gather every year for the Banco
d'Assaggio National Wine Competition
at the Lungarotti estate. Have a glass of
wine at the Osteria del Museo and visit
the museum itself. Don't miss this wine
museum; this is no haphazard collection
of old farming implements. Instead, the
Lungarotti Museum is in a completely
different league. Many of the exhibits
would be just as appropriately housed in
one of the national art museums.

Don't forget the wine, however.
Lungarotti's Vigna Monticchio Rubesco
Riserva and Torgiano Riserva are two
of Italy's finest reds. The company has
long pioneered fine wine making in an
area which is only now emerging from
strictly local importance.

Assisi and Spello
Umbria is full of exquisite medieval
sights. Following the Topino valley
south from Perugia the first stop is
Assisi. It is a tourist trap, but the
Basilica of St Francis is wonderfully
frescoed, with masterpieces of pictorial
narrative by Giotto and many others. It
has such atmosphere that the souvenir
stalls outside fail to ruin it. And, as with
all tourist traps, it is enough to walk
away from the main thoroughfares to

*The pretty hillside wine town of Montefalco, home of
Rosso di Montefalco, is surrounded by its vineyards.*

The Lungarotti wine museum at Torgiano is probably the most important of its kind in Europe. 21 rooms display objects of art and implements of viticulture, ranging from wine presses and wine jars to prints and ceramics by modern and classical artists. Medieval majolica and modern ceramics are impressive, suitably enough for an area of Italy still important today for its artisan-designed ceramics. Engravings and drawings are particularly well represented with artists ranging from Mantegna to Picasso. The collection was started by Maria Grazia Lungarotti, wife of the pioneering winemaker Dr Giorgio Lungarotti.

PIERANTONIO
Az Agrobiologica Colle del Sole* Tel: 075 9414266. Fax: 075 9414390. 0830-1230, 1400-1730. E.F.TF.WS.B.

PILA
Agricola Goretti* Strada del Pino 4. Tel: 075 607316. Fax: 075 6079187. Every day 0830-1300, 1500-1900. E.G.TF.WS.B.

SPELLO
Az Agr F.lli Sportoletti Ernesto e Remo* Via Lombardia 1. Tel/Fax: 0742 651461. Every day 0900-1230, 1500-1900. E.TF.WS. (B for groups).

TORGIANO
Cantine Giorgio Lungarotti* Via Mario Angeloni 16. Tel: 075 9880348. Fax: 075 9880294. 0800-1300, 1500-1800. Osteria del Museo, hotel. E.F. Dutch. TF.WS.B.

MUSEUM
Museo del Vino, Torgiano. Tel: 075 9880200. All year 0900-1300, 1500-1800. Charge for entry.

escape the crowds. Climb up to the castle and peer down through the gunports at the town below if the tourists get too much for you.

Spello, some 6km (4 miles) away has everything: a Roman theatre, Roman gates, and Perugino and Pinturicchio frescoes. Every year at the feast of Corpus Christi, the streets are decorated with mosaics in petals and seeds.

Montefalco

I must declare a personal interest in the wine of Montefalco. My first year in Italy was spent in Foligno (between Montefalco and Spello), a town chiefly known for its railway junction and barracks where, so the conscripts said, the chief activity was cleaning the donkey stables. Foligno's grocery shops offered only two-litre Vino Rosso or 75cl Rosso di Montefalco 1976. Having been brought up on the wines of France, I had no idea what to expect. But I found the Rosso di Montefalco truly superb – yet no one outside the area had heard of it. The year I left,

Rosso di Montefalco was made a DOC wine. Totally unjustifiably, I felt that my constant praise for this wine had something to do with it.

Montefalco is now firmly on the wine map. Sagrantino, a unique local grape variety producing attractive brambly red wines, has gained international recognition. Indeed, Montefalco has now established the National Centre for Passito Wines on the strength of the success of the fine dessert version of this wine, Sagrantino Passito. Like the better known Amarone and Recioto of the Veneto area, the dessert wine can be either sweet or dry and is made from semi-dried grapes pressed about three months after harvest.

Visit Montefalco for its frescoed churches (the Museo Civico San Francesco is superb), its town walls and its medieval atmosphere. Nearby Bevagna is notable for its main square with its two typically Umbrian Romanesque churches that face each other in a dark setting that seems to come straight from a Walter Scott novel.

Food of Central Italy

Central Italy is proud of an inheritance of celebrated and historic wines. This sign outside a wine shop proclaims the classic regional wines. Produzione propria *means that the wine is the shop's own, the produce of its estate.*

PIZZA A TAGLIO

Hungry tourists looking for a quick snack will appreciate one Umbrian facility, the *pizza a taglio* shops which serve pizza by the wedge, freshly cooked and ready for your mid-morning stroll or pre-dinner *passeggiata*. This custom is not specifically Umbrian, but if you have come from the North the shops may not yet be familiar to you – it is difficult to find them outside the tourist areas further north. The further south you go, the more there are of them.

FESTIVALS

February: SPELLO: *Festa dell'Olio e Sagra della Bruschetta* olive oil festival and tasting.

March/April: TODI: National Antiques Fair.

April: GUBBIO (and numerous other Umbrian towns and villages): Good Friday Procession.

April/May: NARNI: *Giostra all'Anello*, jousting.

May: ASSISI: National Antiques Fair.

May: ASSISI: *Calendimaggio*, a medieval fair.

End May: GUBBIO: *Palio della Balestra*, medieval crossbow archery.

May: GUBBIO: *Festa dei Ceri* race.

June: BOLSENA: *Infiorata*, a flower festival on Corpus Christi.

June: ORVIETO: Corpus Christi, a medieval procession.

June: SPELLO: Corpus Christi flower festival.

June/July: SPOLETO: Festival of Two Worlds.

July: GRADOLI: Festival of Aleatico, local wine festival.

August: CITTÀ DELLA PIEVE/CASTIGLIONE DEL LAGO: *Palio dei Terzieri*, a medieval fair.

September: FOLIGNO: *Giostra della Quintana*, a medieval joust.

October/November: GUBBIO: truffle festival.

November: CITTÀ DI CASTELLO: truffle festival.

FOOD SPECIALITIES

Umbrian cuisine is characterized by the freshness of its ingredients and the immediacy of its cooking methods. With a simplicity and rusticity that befits the land of Saint Francis, the spit, the grill and the wood-burning oven are the traditional cooking methods: *alla brace*, *alla griglia*, and *al forno di legno* are the signs to look for.

The fruity green olive oil of Umbria is delicious, and probably shares the honours with the olive oil of Tuscany as the best in Italy. Spello, Spoleto, the Valnerina and Amerino valleys are the centres of production. Spello holds a *Sagra della Bruschetta* (*bruschetta* feast) which is a celebration of toasted Umbrian bread rubbed with garlic and sprinkled with extra-virgin olive oil and salt.

Cinghiale (wild boar) is often on the menu, as are *piccioni* (pigeons) and *uccelletti* (small birds eaten whole, cooked on a spit with bay leafs and chunks of bread to separate them).

The black truffle of Norcia and Spoleto is a prized ingredient, used especially to flavour omelettes. Cheese and salami, and other pork products from Norcia, are also particularly good. In fact, so famous are the pork butchers of Norcia that the word *Norcineria* is used as a generic term in Italy to denote a high-class *salumeria* (pork butcher).

Lentils from Castelluccio are a prized product. The combination of lentils and pigs' ears in a stew sounds unlikely, but for lovers of comfort food it is unbeatable.

Freshwater fish are represented by trout from the pure waters of Fonti di Clitunno, carp from Lake Trasimene, eels and roach.

Other regional dishes include:
Cardi alla perugina: cardoons fried in batter, then cooked in the oven with a *ragù* sauce.
Palombacce all'uso di Foligno: casseroled pigeon cooked with its giblets with olives and vegetables.
Porchetta sucking pig stuffed with garlic, pepper and rosemary, usually bought from wayside vans and eaten in bread rolls.
Scottaditto lamb cutlets, so called because they are meant to be eaten direct from the wood fire, so literally leading to burned fingers.
Stringozzi home-made flat pasta, often served with mushrooms or truffles.

FOR FURTHER INFORMATION

Consorzio Tutela Denominazione Orvieto Classico e Orvieto Corso Cavour 36, 05018 Orvieto. Tel: 0763 43790.

PUBLICATION

Andar per Vigne is the title of a useful pamphlet, in English and Italian, produced by the Consorzio Tutela Denominazione Orvieto giving details of wineries in the area open to visitors.

The Barberani wine shop in Orvieto's cathedral square displays wines of the region.

The Adriatic Coast

The eastern side of the Apennines does not have the same attractions for the traveller as Tuscany or the Veneto, with their obvious cultural delights. It is the motorway-loving holiday-makers who tend to stay on this coast of Italy. Scan the map and very few towns stand out immediately: Urbino, of course, is known for its Ducal Palace; Ancona, for its port; Loreto, for the Santa Casa; Bari, for its famous church of San Nicola; and Brindisi, for its port and the ferry for Greece.

But there is much more to discover: the hill towns of the Marches, the architectural splendour of Ascoli Piceno, the National Park of Abruzzo, the archeological museum of Chieti, Castel del Monte, the *trulli* of Alberobello and the Baroque palaces of Lecce. The people here are different; they are more relaxed and more friendly, and more insular too. The people of Abruzzo are proud of their reputation as *forti e gentili*, hard of purpose but gentle of manner, and the same attributes apply to the Marchigiani and the Pugliesi as well.

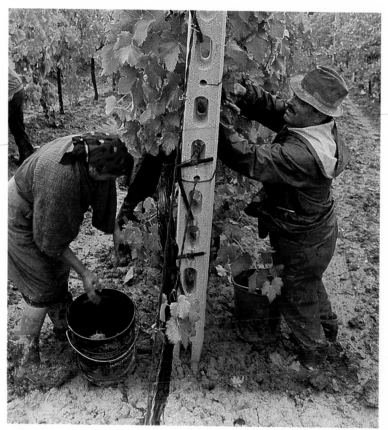

Harvest time for Verdicchio grapes in the Esino Valley.

Politically and vinously the Adriatic coast is divided into three main sections: the Marches; Abruzzo/Molise; and Puglia.

The Marches are the home of the most celebrated Adriatic wine: Verdicchio. The amphora, or Lollobrigida-shaped bottle is a familiar sight on trattoria tables abroad, and this is undoubtedly the best wine to drink with the local fish. Less well known, but perhaps to the connoisseur more interesting, are the two reds of the Marches, Rosso Conero and Rosso Piceno. Other wines of the area are of local interest only. Some producers are making excellent sparkling wines with Verdicchio grapes, and while these are too expensive to compete with other sparkling wines abroad, they are very pleasant to taste during travels in the region.

In Abruzzo there are only three wines: two Montepulciano d'Abruzzos, the red, and the

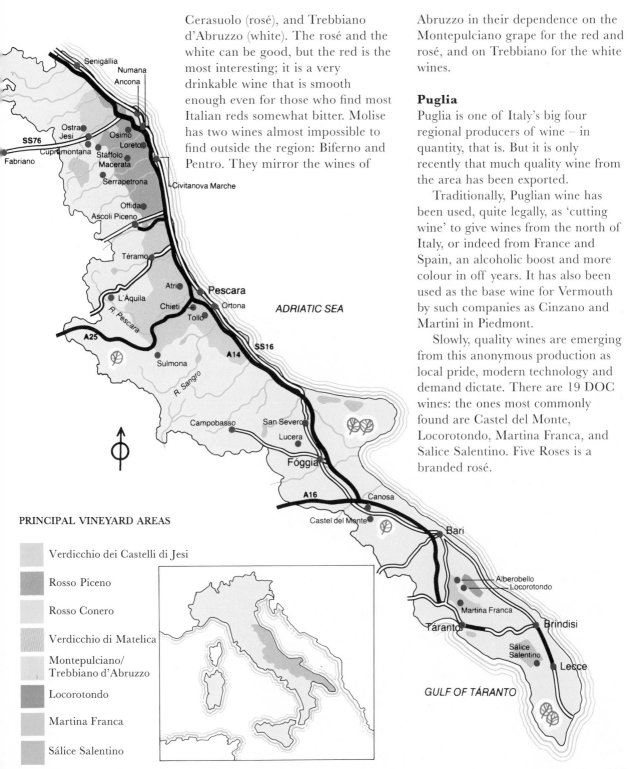

Cerasuolo (rosé), and Trebbiano d'Abruzzo (white). The rosé and the white can be good, but the red is the most interesting; it is a very drinkable wine that is smooth enough even for those who find most Italian reds somewhat bitter. Molise has two wines almost impossible to find outside the region: Biferno and Pentro. They mirror the wines of Abruzzo in their dependence on the Montepulciano grape for the red and rosé, and on Trebbiano for the white wines.

Puglia

Puglia is one of Italy's big four regional producers of wine – in quantity, that is. But it is only recently that much quality wine from the area has been exported.

Traditionally, Puglian wine has been used, quite legally, as 'cutting wine' to give wines from the north of Italy, or indeed from France and Spain, an alcoholic boost and more colour in off years. It has also been used as the base wine for Vermouth by such companies as Cinzano and Martini in Piedmont.

Slowly, quality wines are emerging from this anonymous production as local pride, modern technology and demand dictate. There are 19 DOC wines: the ones most commonly found are Castel del Monte, Locorotondo, Martina Franca, and Salice Salentino. Five Roses is a branded rosé.

ADRIATIC SEA

GULF OF TÁRANTO

PRINCIPAL VINEYARD AREAS

- Verdicchio dei Castelli di Jesi
- Rosso Piceno
- Rosso Conero
- Verdicchio di Matelica
- Montepulciano/ Trebbiano d'Abruzzo
- Locorotondo
- Martina Franca
- Sálice Salentino

The Marches

The Castelli di Jesi hills nourish Verdicchio vineyards and give their name to one of the two versions of the wine.

The best way to travel along the length of the Adriatic coast is to use the A14 motorway as a vertical axis, and only cut inland as necessary.

Urbino

Coming south from Romagna, the first diversion will be inland to Urbino. The vast hilltop Ducal Palace dates mainly from the mid 15th century, when Federigo da Montefeltro, a great warrior and a notable patron of art, ruled the city. The palace has wonderful views over the countryside, and it contains the National Gallery of the Marches.

The wines of the area are the white Bianchello del Metauro and the red Sangiovese dei Colli Pesaresi – both are light wines of local interest.

Verdicchio

The best known wine of the Marches is Verdicchio. There are, in fact, two Verdicchios; Verdicchio di Matelica is the rarer one and comes from near Fabriano; Verdicchio dei Castelli di Jesi is the well-known one that comes in the amphora-shaped bottle.

Verdicchio has been called variously 'the Muscadet of Italy' by admirers of its fresh and steely style and 'the Burgundy of Italy' by those who want to invest it with the nobility of oak ageing. (Try Umani Ronchi's Le Busche or Garofoli's Serra Fiorese for successful versions of this unusual style).

The wine is made from the grape of the same name. As a still wine, it is capable of more character than its nearest rivals, Frascati and Soave. As a sparkling wine, it already has a long tradition; it may have been French troops who introduced the idea to the area at the time of the Napoleonic Kingdom of Italy.

The future of Verdicchio seems more secure with each successive improvement in quality. First, there was cold fermentation, which improved the natural fruitiness of the wine. Then there were decisions to create superior *cuvée* examples of Verdicchio by reducing yields in the vineyards (thereby picking fewer but better quality grapes); making special grape selections from individual vineyards known to be particularly favourably sited; late harvesting (to concentrate the sugars and richness in the grapes naturally); and cold maceration to build structure and depth in the wine. Some even age Verdicchio on the lees (one of the more valid comparisons with Muscadet).

Certainly there is no better wine to accompany the local fish and white meats than crisp, fruity Verdicchio.

The castles of Jesi

The Castelli di Jesi of the Verdicchio wine appellation are the small hill towns surrounding Jesi to the north, south and west. In the times when the Marches were a troubled border area, these satellite fortified towns owed allegiance to Jesi, a garrison town of massive fortifications, now with handicraft and other shops in the alleys of the old fortifications.

Several of the Castelli di Jesi towns are worth visiting. Local food specialities such as *Tagliatelle alla porchetta* are well suited to Verdicchio. Cupramontana is the acknowledged 'Capital of Verdicchio' and has an International Museum of Wine Labels. Staffolo has superb views over neighbouring hill towns; the church of San Francesco al Musone is reputedly where St Francis halted to pray on his way to Ancona.

North of Jesi there is Morro d'Alba with its own robust red DOC wine, Lacrima di Morro d'Alba. An interesting walk can be had in the 17th-century walkway around the town walls.

The main road from Ancona westwards is signposted 'Roma 310km'! Stop at Fabriano for its Paper Museum and medieval town centre, and to taste the wines of Mecvini.

Rosso Conero and Piceno

There are two important red wines in the Marches, both intended for ageing. Rosso Conero comes from Mount Conero just south of Ancona, and is proof of the suitability of the Montepulciano grape, its principal

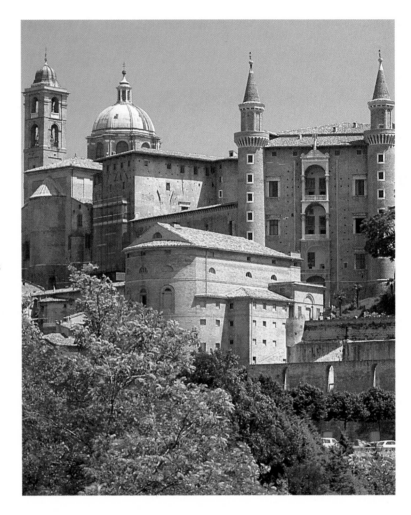

constituent, to the area. For a prize-winning *barrique* version of this wine try Umani Ronchi's Cùmaro, or, for something more traditional, try Le Terazze's offering. A new *Strada del Vino* route has just been laid out in the Rosso Conero area.

Rosso Piceno Superiore, which can be like a Chianti Riserva, comes from the Tronto valley further down the coast. Don't miss Ascoli Piceno with its wealth of medieval and Renaissance buildings, or the pretty hills around Offida where the Strada del Rosso Piceno leads the traveller past several wineries on the way back to the coast.

Urbino's Ducal Palace commands wonderful views over the countryside and contains the National Gallery of the Marches.

The neck label of Rosso Conero (below) features the Roman triumphal arch at Ancona built by the emperor Trajan.

Abruzzo and Molise

ABRUZZO

BOLOGNANO
Az Agr Ciccio Zaccagnini* Contrada Pozzo. Tel: 085 8880195. Fax: 085 8880288. (Marcello Zaccagnini). 1000-1300,1500-1700. F.TF.WS.B.

CONTROGUERRA
Az. Vit. Dino Illuminati* Contrada S. Biagio 18. Tel: 0861 856631/810064. Fax: 0861 810004. (Stefano Illuminati, Agostino Capecci). 0800-1200, 1500-1800. E.G.TF.WS.B.
Az Agr Camillo Montori* Via Piane Tronto 80. Tel: 0861 809900. Fax: 0861 809912. (Camillo Montori). Museum. F.G.TF.WS.

NOTARESCO
Fattoria Bruno Nicodemi* Contrada Veniglio. Tel: 085 895493. Fax: 085 8958887. (Bruno Nicodemi). 0800-1700. E.F.TF.WS.B.

TOLLO
Cantina Tollo scarl* Via Garibaldi 68. Tel: 0871 961726. Fax: 0871 962122. (Sig Agostini or Sig Giannantonio). 0800-1200, 1400-1800. TF.WS.B.

TORANO NUOVO
Az Agr Barone Cornacchia* Le Torri. Tel: 0861 87412. Fax: 0861 88008. (Paola Cornacchia). 0800-1200, 1500-1800. E.F.S.TF.WS.b.
Az Agr Pepe* Via Chiesi 10. Tel/Fax: 0861 856493. (Stefania Pepe). E.F.S.TF. (TP for full tasting or tasting with typical foods). WS.B.

Until the building of the motorway from Rome, Abruzzo was more or less cut off from the rest of Italy. This was part of its charm, and the reason travellers came to discover the self-reliant Abruzzesi people with their reputation for being *forti e gentili*, or rather rough but honest.

Indeed, once the English gentleman or lady of means had explored the civilizing effects of Venice, Florence and Rome, the Abruzzi, as it was called, was the next stop, to discover some of the worthy values of a sturdy peasantry and some of their folklore (the Procession of the Snake-catchers in Cocullo every May never failed to impress then and still takes place today).

Edward Lear, the Victorian artist, traveller and nonsense rhymer, painted a large series of watercolours of this region he so admired.

Right up to the 1970s this was definitely part of the poor Mezzogiorno, the backward South of Italy. But since the motorway came the area has gained new wealth, and Abruzzo now has the highest per capita income of the Mezzogiorno.

Abruzzo's three wines
In wine terms, Abruzzo has the highest percentage of DOC wines in southern Italy, but in terms of quantity it is a long way behind Sicily and Puglia.

After the complexities of other areas it is a relief to come across a region where there are only three names to remember.

Montepulciano d'Abruzzo is a smooth red wine with an attractive earthy nose, and is particularly good value; it can be aged for up to about five years. It is made from the

Montepulciano grape (not to be confused with the Tuscan wine Vino Nobile di Montepulciano).

If the skins are extracted from the fermentation process soon after it has begun, a rosé wine results, and Montepulciano d'Abruzzo Cerasuolo takes its name from its cherry-like colour. It is a pleasantly dry wine and should be drunk while still young.

The third wine of the region is the white Trebbiano d'Abruzzo. Often the Trebbiano grape produces dull and flat wines. In Abruzzo, however, the whites tend to be more characterful and fuller bodied. Valentini is the most famous producer.

The wine roads
Abruzzo has the benefits of mountains, hills and beach resorts all within a short distance of each other. Skiing, sight-seeing and swimming are all possible in a single day. It is in the hills just inland from the sea that the vineyards are to be found.

Just over the border from the Marches, the hilly town of Controguerra has panoramic views over the surrounding countryside. This area is Abruzzo's finest, so much so that the producers of the province of Teramo are currently in the process of applying for a separate denomination in a bid to distance themselves from the mass market wines that come from some of the co-operatives further down the coast. They have their own *Strada del Vino delle Colline Teramane* (Wine Road of the Teramo Hills) with many wineries that welcome visitors.

Atri to Chieti

On your way southwards on the coastal route, stop at the hill town of Atri. The town has an ancient past. It has a frescoed cathedral built on Roman foundations – indeed the Adriatic Sea may well derive its name from the town's old Roman name, Hadria Picena.

Most of the wine in Abruzzo comes from the province of Chieti. If you have time, try to visit the town for its Roman remains, and for the archeological museum with its prize exhibit, the extraordinary 6th-century BC statue known as the Warrior of Capestrano.

The town of Celano in Abruzzo with its imposing 15th-century castle bears witness to Abruzzo's military past.

Molise

Once considered secondary to the wines of Abruzzo, Molise has recently gained administrative independence. This is remote and attractively rural countryside, and several traditional industries live on here: lace, carpets, ceramics and terracotta, for example.

The two DOC wines of Molise, Pentro and Biferno, are made in similar styles to the wines of Abruzzo.

The Di Majo Norante winery at Campomarino on the coast has represented serious wines from Molise since the company's relaunch in 1968. The range of wines is wide: a Sangiovese, a Montepulciano, an Aglianico, a Trebbiano, and a Malvasia are made alongside wines from other more unusual grapes, such as Falanghina, Greco, and Fiano – staples of quality winemaking in the Campania area but more unusual on this side of Italy.

MOLISE

CAMPOMARINO

Az Agr Di Majo Norante C. da Ramitelli 4. Tel: 0875 57208. Fax: 0875 57379. (Alessio Di Majo). 0900-1300, 1400-1800. E.TF.WS.B.

Puglia

ANDRIA
Az Vin Rivera* SS 98
Km 19,800 Contrada
Rivera. Tel: 0883 541310.
Fax: 083 563679. (Carlo de
Corato, Leonardo
Palumbo). 0900-1700.
E.F.TF.WS.B.
Enoteca Pellegrino Via
Firenze 53. Tel: 0883
559727.
**Enoteca Giuseppe de
Corato** Via S Rosa 71.
Tel: 0883 563318.

GUAGNANO
Az Agr Cosimo Taurino
SS605. Tel: 0832 706490.
Fax: 0832 706242.
(Francesco or Rosanna
Taurino). 0800-1300.
E.TF.WS.B.

SÁLICE SALENTINO
**Ant Az Agr Vit Conti
Leone de Castris*** Via
Senatore de Castris 50.
Tel: 0832 731112. Fax:
0832 731114. (Leonardo
Pinto). 0830-1230.
Museum of winemaking
implements. E.TF.WS. (B
for groups.)

Puglia has always produced vast quantities of wine, up to one fifth of Italian production. Strangely enough, it is is now producing some of Italy's most exciting wines. The new supermarket wines that might be descibed as having 'bags of jammy fruit' (reds) or 'luscious peachiness' (whites) are now coming from Puglia, often marketed as 'made with the help of Australian wine-makers'. Consequently these wines are largely made to order for the supermarket export trade and not seen in the region at all.

Luckily, there are some producers, Taurino, Leone de Castris and Rivera among them, who produce wines that are internationally famous and can be discovered in Puglia as well.

There are over 20 DOC appellations and several *Vini a Indicazione Geografica Tipica*.

Puglia's wine roads

Travelling south along the A14 Adriatic motorway one of the first towns encountered is Lucera. Lucera reflects the epochs of Puglia's importance with its Roman amphitheatre, Swabian castle and Angevin cathedral. Its wine is a tongue-twister: *Cacc'e mmitte di Lucera* – the dialect name apparently means 'drink and pour again'.

Puglia is rich in Roman and in early medieval history. Near Canosa is Canne della Battaglia – Cannae, where Hannibal was defeated by the Romans in 216 BC. Canosa itself has two masterpieces of Puglian art in the 11th-century bishop's throne and pulpit in the cathedral.

Rosso Canosa is one of the three local reds: the others are Rosso di Barletta and Rosso di Cerignola. An unusual wine of the area is Moscato di Trani, which is a sweet muscat, excellent with fruit.

Locorotondo (above) is one of the most splendid 'white towns' of the Puglian plains. It produces its own DOC wine, as does its neighbour Martina Franca.

The finest monument to Puglia's Golden Age is the Castel del Monte, a short distance south-east of Canosa. It was built as a hunting lodge by the Emperor Frederick II around 1240 and has a distinctive octagonal design. Castel del Monte gives its name to the DOC wine whose most famous exponent is the Rivera company in Andria. They are well known for their rosé; their best wine is a Riserva called Il Falcone.

The *Trulli*

Midway between Bari and Brindisi is Alberobello and the zone of the *trulli*. These conical-roofed peasant dwellings originated as an easy method of house building; the local rocks easily split into thin layers, ideal for dry stone wall construction. In the time of the Bourbon rule, when new houses were taxable, this construction meant they were easily dismantled if necessary. Locorotondo, Ostuni, and Martina Franca are the three local whites.

Lecce and Táranto

In the heel of Italy is the lovely Baroque town of Lecce. Nearby are the DOC wine areas of Sálice Salentino, Leverano and Alezio. The rosé versions are very successful: Rosa del Golfo from Giuseppe Calò and Five Roses from Leone de Castris especially. Five Roses acquired its name during the war when American soldiers apparently rated it more highly than a well-known Bourbon.

Between Lecce and Táranto is Manduria, home of the Primitivo grape that is perhaps the origin of California's Zinfandel. The wine is a formidably strong red which can be sweet and fortified, too.

Táranto is well worth a visit. It was the most important city in the Greek colony of Magna Graecia and has an important archeological museum.

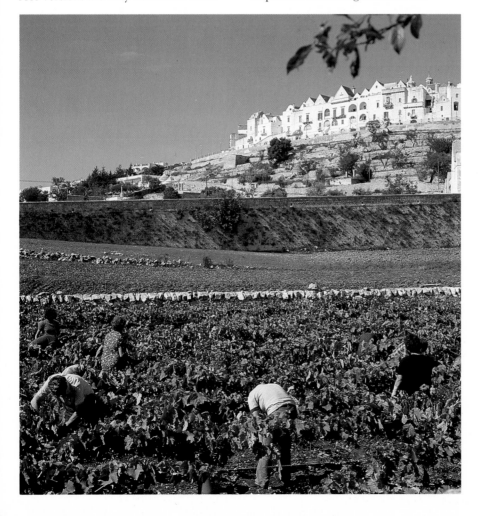

Harvesting in the vineyards around Locorotondo. The local co-operative is responsible for the international fame of its uncomplicated white wine.

Food of the Adriatic Coast

FOR FURTHER INFORMATION

Ente Provinciale per il Turismo Via B Spaventa 29, Chieti. Tel: 0871 63640. Fax: 0871 63647.

Ente Provinciale per il Turismo Via del Castello 10, Teramo. Tel: 0861 244222 Fax: 0861 244357. Information includes interesting booklet, *English Travellers in Abruzzo 1838-1914*.

FOOD SPECIALITIES

The Marches

The cuisine of the Marches is ingenuous and uncomplicated; dishes are cooked in a simple manner, reflecting the naturally healthy Mediterranean diet.

Some specialities:
Brodetto: fish stew, traditionally with as many fish as there are apostles.
Vincisgrassi: owes its name to an Austrian prince who stopped in Ancona in Napoleonic times, Prince Windisch-Gratz; baked lasagne with chicken liver and white sauce.
Stoccafisso all'Anconitana: stewed stockfish.
Trippa alla canapina: tripe from Jesi.
Game from Loreto.
Salami from Fabriano.
Olive ripiene all'ascolana: large stuffed and deep-fried green olives.

Abruzzo Molise

The most famous dish of Abruzzo is *Maccheroni alla chitarra*, made by stretching a thin sheet of fresh pasta over a frame with wires like guitar strings that cuts the pasta into strips. The sauce is meat- or tomato-based.

As in all the Adriatic coastal regions there is a version of *brodetto*, fish soup, adapted to the local catch. Fish is regarded more highly than meat in this region.

The traditional cheese used to flavour pasta dishes is often *pecorino* (sheep's cheese) rather than parmesan. It goes especially well with lamb and vegetable-based sauces.

Some specialities:
Orecchie di preti: priests' ears pasta.
Scripelle imbussi: pancakes filled with cheese and ham.

Trippa alla paesana: tripe with hot peppers and tomatoes.

Puglia

The cuisine of Puglia is based on simple products and strong flavours. The most famous pasta of Puglia are the ear-shaped *orecchiette*.

The coast provides fresh fish and shellfish: anchovies, mussels, squid and oysters particularly.

Lamb is very important, reflecting the fact that Puglia is the third most important region for sheep farming after Lazio and Sardinia.

Some specialities:
Annulieddu a lu furnu (Agnello al forno): baby lamb and potato casserole.
Calzengfiidde: small *calzone*, or pizza envelope, filled with meat or cheese.
Ciambotto: pasta sauce made of tiny fish with onions and tomatoes.
Cozze gratinate: baked mussels.
Melanzane ripiene: stuffed aubergines.
Pepperoni arrotolati: stuffed peppers.
Zuppa di pesce alla gallipolina: fish stew with a little tomato and vinegar.

FESTIVALS

Marches

Easter Monday: SAN MARCELLO: sausage and salami festival.
May: MONTECAROTTO: fish and Verdicchio festival.
First Sunday of June: SAN MARCELLO: *Palio Sanmarcellese*, folk festival.
July and August: NUMANA: Rosso Conero and Verdicchio exhibition.
First Sunday of August: STAFFOLO: festival.
August: PESARO: Rossini Festival.
August: ROSORA: festival of Verdicchio.
September: ASCOLI PICENO: *Giostra della Quintana*, medieval joust and Renaissance costume procession.

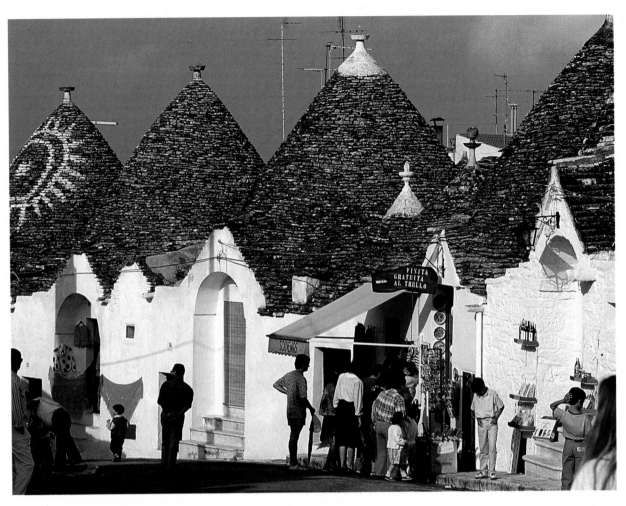

Last Sunday of September: ARCEVIA: *festa dell'uva (*wine festival).
First Sunday of October: CUPRAMONTANA: *festa dell'uva* and wine exhibition.

Abruzzo Molise

January: RIVISONDOLI: *Presepe Vivente*, nativity scene.
Easter: L'AQUILA: Good Friday Procession.
Easter Sunday: SULMONA: *Madonna che scapa in piazza* procession.
May, first Thursday: COCULLO: procession of the Serpari in which a statue of St Dominic is paraded adorned with live snakes.
August: MONTEPAGANO: wine festival.
August: ORTONA: *Rassegna Regionale dei Vin*i, regional wine festival.
August: BASCIAMO: *prosciutto* (ham) festival.
September: ORTONA: mullet festival.

Puglia

May: BARI: Feast of St Nicholas procession recalls the arrival of the bones of the Saint in 1087.
September: MASSAFRA: *Palio della Mezzaluna* celebrates a battle against the Saracens.

Tourism has become important for the trulli – conical-roofed peasant dwellings – in Alberobello at Locorotondo (see pages 116-117).

The Mediterranean Coast

The further south you travel the deeper you are in the Mezzogiorno, Italy's most poverty-stricken and depressed region. This is the home of those who have perfected the *arte di arrangiarsi*, the art of getting by, by hook or by crook. It is no accident that Naples, with its high unemployment, has a thriving underground economy, and horrifying crime levels. Yet this is a city packed with wonderful churches, Roman, medieval and Baroque, and with a glorious ancient past still manifest in its ruins and museums. (Rome is untypical; ancient, proud and bureaucratic, with great treasures and impossible traffic.)

Four regions are involved. Lazio is divided by Rome, south of which the Mezzogiorno begins. Campania's salvation is the tourism of Naples, Capri, Ischia and the Amalfi coast. Basilicata, in the instep of Italy, is very poor. Calabria's hope and challenge is the tourism the motorways bring.

The Spanish Steps in Rome, one of countless monuments to the city's Baroque splendour. The English Romantic poet John Keats died in 1821 in a house overlooking the stairway.

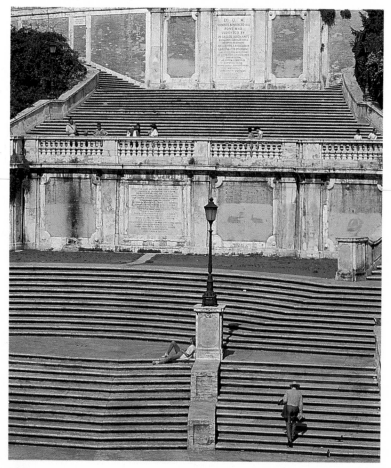

Lazio

Until the beginning of the present century, Rome was surrounded by deserted and malaria-ridden countryside, except for the Colli Albani hills to the south-east. Here, amidst the summer villas of the Roman aristocracy, the predominantly white wines of the region are produced. Frascati is the most famous, but each hill town has its own wine. Some are DOC: Marino, Montecompatri and Velletri, for example, as well as Frascati. These are clean and simple wines; if they have any striking feature, it is the bitter almond twist to the aftertaste.

Wine is also made north of Rome, around Cervéteri, and between the Colli Albani and the coast, on the plains drained by Mussolini near Aprilia. The Merlot of Aprilia can be very good.

Campania

The resorts of Capri and Ischia produce their own wines, as much to preserve the typical landscape of these beauty spots as to make a reasonable wine. From vineyards around Mount Vesuvius comes the famous Lacrima Christi, the name invented by local monks.

But the great wines of Campania are in Avellino: the whites Greco di Tufo and Fiano di Avellino, and the outstanding red Taurasi. These are still very little known.

Falernum is one of the wines of Ancient Rome. It survives today as Falerno, albeit in a different form to the smoky wine that the Romans liked to dilute with water – three parts to one of wine.

Basilicata

The claim to vinous fame of this forgotten region is a wine that is well known amongst Italian wine lovers: Aglianico del Vulture. Most often this is a strong red suitable for ageing, like Barolo, for example.

Calabria

Two wines stand out here: Cirò, which can be red, white or rosé; and the sweet white Greco di Bianco, from the town of Bianco, on the toe of Italy.

PRINCIPAL VINEYARD AREAS

- Est! Est!! Est!!!
- Frascati
- Velletri
- Greco di Tufo
- Taurasi
- Aglianico del Vulture
- Cirò

Frascati and the Colli Albani

Frascati is the name that everyone recognizes. It is a clean, but slightly rich tasting pale white, with a touch of almond flavour on the aftertaste. It must be drunk young, no older than two vintages.

Frascati – the town

Frascati is one of a semicircle of towns around the Colli Albani hills. The hills are, in fact, extinct volcanoes, and the two lakes, Albano and Nemi, are water-filled craters. Lake Nemi was known as the Mirror of Diana in classical times, because of the pagan temple sited on its shores.

The town of Frascati is almost a suburb of Rome, but its splendid villas witness the popularity it enjoyed as a retreat for the Roman aristocracy. Villa Aldobrandini and the monument to Bonnie Prince Charlie in the cathedral of San Pietro are worth seeing.

Wines of the Colli Albani

Frascati is only one of the wines produced in the Colli Albani area, also south-east of Rome. The others, all whites with pretty similar characteristics, are Marino, Colli Albani, Colli Lanuvini, Montecompatri Colonna, Velletri and Zagarolo. Velletri, unusually, is also made as a quaffable red wine that is usually very good value.

Using the side roads, it is a pleasant drive to turn off the A2 motorway at Monteporzio Catone, where many of the Frascati producers are based, and then follow the roads around the Colli Albani hills to Velletri.

Grottaferrata and Castel Gandolfo

Grottaferrata has panoramic views and an 11th-century Byzantine abbey. Marino is a little town above the shores of Lake Albano, and its wine is next to Frascati in popularity.

COLONNA
Pallavicini* Via Casilina Km25,500, Colonna. Tel/Fax: 06 9438816. (Roberta Malatesta). 1100-1700. Group visits to winery and restaurant. TP.WS.B.

FRASCATI
Az Agr Casale Marchese* Via di Vermicino. Tel/Fax: 06 9408932. (Alessandro Carletti). E.F.TF.WS.B.
Az Agr L'Olivella Via di Colle Pisano 5. Tel: 06 9424527 Fax: 06 9425656. (Umberto Notarnicola). Old grotto. E.TP.WS.B.
Tenuta di Pietra Porzia* Via Prataporci 60. Tel: 06 9464392. Fax: 06 9464361. (Giuseppe Santini). 1000-1900. TP.WS.b.
Cantine Conte Zandotti* Tel: 06 20609000. Fax: 06 20609045. (Sig.ra Bellante). Cellars in a 2nd-century BC Roman cistern. E.F.S.TP.WS.B.

The wines of Lazio in general do not have a strong character; they are quite unlike the masculine, opaque reds of Piedmont or the delicate feminine wines of the Veneto. Instead, the whites of Lazio, and its few reds, are often impersonal, despite their attractive drinkability. In other words, they are wines to be enjoyed rather than examined critically.

Frascati – the wine

For 2000 years the Castelli Romani hills south-east of Rome have been the recreational resort of the Romans. Cicero had a villa at Tuscolo, and tradition has it that Cato lived at Monteporzio Catone. Colli di Tuscolo and Villa di Catone are wine brands that recall this heritage. It is a delightful area, but try to avoid the Roman holidays.

It is still possible to find the traditional rustic *osteria*, where pitchers of local wine can be enjoyed outside at a table sheltered from the sun that Rome seems to bask in for much of the year. What could be better than a glass of cold Frascati and a *panino* of pork and rosemary?

Just around the shores of the lake is Castel Gandolfo, the Pope's famous private residence and ancient site of Alba Longa.

Between the Colli Albani hills and the coast are the plains of Aprilia. Locals claim that the Trebbiano, Merlot and Sangiovese di Aprilia should be excellent, as the climate is similar to California's. My own favourite is the fruity red Merlot.

Left: An elaborate sculpted fountain at Frascati, near the town hall.

Below: Not far from Frascati is the Abbey of San Nilo at Grottaferrata.

GROTTAFERRATA
Az Agr Castel de Paolis* Via Val de Paolis. Tel: 06 9413648. Fax: 06 94316025. (Giulio Santarelli). 1000-1300, 1700-1900. E.TF.WS.B.

ARICCIA
Cantine Volpetti srl* Via Nettunense 21 Km 7,800. Tel: 06 9342000. Fax: 06 9342941. (Mauro Volpetti). 0800-1700. E.TP.WS.B.

MONTEPORZIO CATONE
Cantine Colli di Catone Via Frascati 31-33. Tel: 06 9449113. Fax: 06 9448695. (Carla Pulcini). 0900-1300, 1500-1800. E.TP.WS.B.
Az Agr Piero Costantini Via Frascati – Colonna 29. Tel: 06 9449717. Fax: 06 9448658. (Lorenzo Costantini). E.TP.WS.B.
Fontana Candida Via di Fontana Candida 11. Tel: 06 9420066. Fax: 06 9448591. 0830-1300, 1400-1700. TF.B.
Cantine San Marco Via di Frascati 60. Tel: 06 9422689. Fax: 06 9425333. (Umberto Notarnicola). 0900-1230, 1330-1700. E.TP.WS.B.

ROME
Enoteca Trimani Via Goito 20. Tel: 06 497971. Daily 0900-1300, 1600-2000. Marco Trimani is one of the greatest publicists of Italian wine.

Anagni

On the A2, about 20km (12 miles) before Frosinone, Anagni has a superb Romanesque cathedral as well as Cesanese del Piglio, an unusual red in several styles: dry for long ageing; *amabile* (medium sweet); and *dolce* (sweet). Anagni is also the home of one of Italy's finest red wines, Torre Ercolana, an unusual but highly successful blend of Cabernet, Merlot and Cesanese grapes made on the Colacicchi estate by Marco Trimani, one of the greatest enthusiasts in the Italian wine world and owner of the Enoteca Trimani wine shop in the centre of Rome.

Campania

Campania has two faces: one is the traditional jolly image of Italy, spaghetti and pizza, holidays on Capri and Positano, gaiety, dance and song.

The other face is the high unemployment of Naples, the viciousness of its Mafia, the Camorra, and the extensive destruction still evident from the 1980 earthquake.

Wine in this land has a very ancient tradition. The Greeks who colonized southern Italy before Roman times were so struck with the vine-growing potential here that they called their colony Enotria, which comes from Greek *oinos*, and also gives us the word 'wine'. Ischia, whose wine was awarded the first DOC in Campania, was once known as Enaria, 'the land of wine'.

The Greek tradition lingers today in several wine names: Greco di Tufo, Greco di Somma, Vino Greco; and the major red wine grape of Campania and Basilicata called Aglianico derives from *hellenico*, 'the Greek one'.

The two islands off the Gulf of Naples, Ischia and Capri, each produce their own red and white wines. On Ischia, the D'Ambra company plays a leading role in preserving the agricultural heritage of the island and makes its Biancolella wine from an authentic *cru* site in an area under constant threat from the pressures of tourism.

Vesuvius is the site of vineyards that grow the Lacrima Christi (meaning 'Tear of Christ') del Vesuvio. This red, white and rosé wine is mainly famous for its name, but in the hands of a good producer it is respectable enough.

In the hinterland behind Naples are the best wines of Campania. A turning off the A16 motorway leads to Atripalda, where Mastroberardino has its cellars. If anyone deserves the credit for the fame of the wines of this

area abroad, it is Antonio Mastroberardino, who has put these otherwise obscure wines on the map. Fiano di Avellino and Greco di Tufo are the whites. The red is called Taurasi. It is made of the Aglianico grape and capable of great ageing.

IN PRAISE OF FALERNUM

Legend has it that Bacchus, in disguise as a poor man, asked a peasant near Mount Massico for some refreshment. The peasant was so generous that Bacchus turned his homely milk into a wonderful wine – and Falernum was the peasant's name.

The ancient Romans loved the wine Falernum, and it was made to withstand long ageing. In fact, the Romans were sophisticated in their treatment of wine, and used both corks and glass bottles. The Emperor Tiberius is said to have had the inventor of an allegedly unbreakable glass put to death, for fear of ruining the economy.

It is unlikely, however, that Roman wine would have been suitable to modern tastes. For keeping purposes it was often reduced to a concentrated syrupy liquid, and then re-constituted with seawater and flavoured with honey and spices.

The new Falerno is made just over the border from Lazio into Campania, where Villa Matilde have made a speciality out of re-interpreting classical Falernum in the light of current winemaking practices. They have now established themselves as one of Campania's top producers, making wines in an extremely modern style.

Other producers have now followed Mastroberardino's lead in the area, notably Ocone (who makes strictly organic wines under the new DOC Taburno), Vadiaperti (founded by History Professor, Antonio Troisi) and Mustilli. The Mustilli cellars are right in the centre of Sant'Agata dei Goti, a wonderful medieval town, and are run by Leonardo Mustilli with the help of his daughter Paola. The company, which has recently launched an *agriturismo* holiday centre as well, makes wines only from its own vineyards.

Basilicata and Calabria

Vines on bamboo poles in Aglianico vineyards, with Mount Vulture in the background.

BASILICATA

Casa Vinicola D'Angelo
Via Provinciale 8, 85028
Rionero in Vulture (PZ).
Tel: 0972 721517. Fax:
0972 723495. (Donato
D'Angelo). Near castle of
Emperor Frederick II at
Castelagopesole. E.TF.WS.B.

CALABRIA

Librandi C. da S
Gennaro, SS 106, Cirò
Marina (CZ). Tel: 0962
31518. Fax: 0962 370542.
(Nicodemo Librandi).
0830-1300,1500-1800.
E.F.TF.WS.B.

Az Agr Odoardi Viale
della Repubblica 143,
87100 Cosenza. Tel: 0984
29961. Fax: 0984 28503.
(Dr Gregorio Odoardi).
E.F.TF.WS.B.

Called Lucania under the pre-war
Fascist government, Basilicata only
acquired its present name in 1947.

This remote region is movingly
described in Carlo Levi's famous
autobiographical story *Christ Stopped at
Eboli*. Eboli itself is in Campania, but
Levi's experience was of Basilicata,
where he was 'exiled' by the Fascists,
and indeed he is buried there. His
painting *Lucania 1961* is on display at
the Centro Levi in Matera.

Don't miss the Sassi area of Matera
where dwellings and churches cut into
the rock have been occupied since
prehistoric times.

Basilicata wines
Only one wine is DOC and in the
league of great Italian wines: Aglianico
del Vulture. This red wine is made in
several versions: *Riserva* (five years old),
Vecchio (three years old), *Spumante*
(sparkling), and *Amabile* (a sweet dessert
wine).

Aglianico is made in the northern
tip of Basilicata in the area around
Mount Vulture. Visit Fratelli d'Angelo
in Rionero; they are amongst the best
producers of Aglianico.

The deep southern toe of Italy has
its economic and social problems. Until
recently, emigration from Calabria was
the usual course for its young people.

However, the discovery of the
spectacular Bronzes of Riace, ancient
sculptures found on the sea bed off the
coast of Calabria, has done much to
restore local pride; they are now one of
the best reasons to visit the town of
Reggio di Calabria.

Calabrian wines
Most of the Calabrian wines you may
find in the area itself are entirely
unexceptional. But it is an area that
has started to attract interest in the
wine world, especially through the
work of consultant enologist Severino
Garofano, who advises several wineries
in Calabria and in Puglia. Librandi's
Gravello, for example, a blend of the
local Gaglioppo grape with Cabernet
Sauvignon, is one of the Garofano
creations and is regarded as one of
southern Italy's best wines.

Cirò has recently acquired a good
reputation as an uncomplicated red,
white or rosé. It comes from the town
on the western coast of Calabria, and
can claim to be one of the oldest wines
in the world. When southern Italy and
Sicily were part of Magna Graecia, the
Cremissa wine of this area was, so we
are told, awarded to victorious
Olympic athletes.

Further down the coast, almost on
the toe of Italy, is the town of Bianco.
Greco di Bianco and Mantonico di
Bianco are two dessert white wines
with ancient origins and, supposedly,
strong aphrodisiac qualities. Visit the
area for its archeological heritage too –
nearby Locri has impressive Greek
temple remains.

Food of the Mediterranean Coast

FOOD SPECIALITIES

Lazio

Sheep farming was once more important than agriculture to the inhabitants of Lazio. *Abbacchio* is milk-fed spring lamb; *Scottadito* (literally 'finger-burner') is grilled cutlets; *Brodetto alla Romana* is a lamb stew with a sauce flavoured with lemon and thickened with egg.

Lazio is also the home of several internationally famous dishes: *Spaghetti alla carbonara* – with diced bacon, egg yolk and parmesan; *Spaghetti all' Amatriciana* – with tomatoes, bacon, onion and garlic; *Saltimbocca* – beef olives with sage and *prosciutto* (raw ham); and *Stracciatella* – consommé, beaten egg and cheese. Rice is not used, except for the curiously named dish *Suppli al telefono*, rice croquettes filled with mozzarella, whose stringiness provides the reference to telephones.

Campania

Naples is the home of spaghetti and of pizza. Both of these foods are essentially peasant foods and the sauces and toppings tend to be much as they were intended to be: simple. The *spaghetti al pomodoro* tends to have a typical slightly watery sauce.

The best pizzas are cooked in an open wood-fired oven (look for the sign *forno a legno*); a *calzone* is a pizza envelope with a filling rather than a topping; *Pizza alla Napoletana* has a topping of anchovies, tomatoes, and mozzarella flavoured with basil and oregano.

Basilicata: cheese and peppers

From classical times, ancient Lucania has been known for its cheeses: *Provola*, *Caciocavallo* and *Scamorze* are good examples.

The cooking is based very much on local vegetables. Hot and sweet peppers, aubergines, beans, pulses, and lentils, which are cooked in olive oil and flavoured with herbs – these are the essential ingredients.

Calabria

The rites of preserving vegetables are still observed in Calabria. Aubergines, olives, tomatoes and mushrooms all benefit from the southern sun.

Fish, especially trout (*trota*) and swordfish (*pesce spada*), and lamb are also popular. Pasta has many shapes, each with its local name.

FESTIVALS

February: NAPLES: feast of San Gennaro; liquefaction of the blood.
Easter: CATANZARO, NOCERA TERINESE, PROCIDA: Good Friday processions.
May: POTENZA: Cavalcade of the Turks.
July: MATERA: Materano Arts Festival.

An Enoteca in Rome displays fine champagnes as well as Italian wines. Champagne and whisky are both surprisingly popular in Italy, which is the largest market for malt whisky in the world.

Sicily

SICILIAN FOOD

Sicilian cuisine has two sources: one is the tradition of eastern Sicily around Catania, the other of western Sicily around Palermo. The eastern tradition was established in Sicily 2000 years ago, when the island had a well-established cooking school. Fortunately, some authentic Sicilian recipes have survived the onslaught of tourism: *Pasta ci' li sarde:* thick spaghetti-type pasta with tomatoes and fresh sardines. *Pasta ca Norma:* pasta (spaghetti or *penne* usually) with tomato sauce, slices of fried aubergine and ricotta, a soft sheep's milk cheese. The dish is a homage to the opera *Norma* (its composer Bellini came from Catania). *Cassata:* a mould of ricotta, candied fruit, chocolate, flavoured with Maraschino and vanilla.

The theatre at Taormina is part of Sicily's Ancient Greek heritage.

Sicily has always been the property of some other nation. Greeks, Phoenicians, Romans, and Goths, then Byzantines, Moors, Normans and Swabians, French, and Spaniards have held sway over the island from one age to another. Even today, the somewhat inward-looking mentality of Sicilians makes it hard to integrate the island with the mainland. The Temple of Apollo and Artemis in Syracuse is Sicily's history in microcosm: built by the ancient Greeks, subsequently it became a Byzantine church, a Saracen mosque, a Norman church and a Spanish barracks.

Palermo, the capital, has Norman and Baroque monuments, and a medieval palace with glittering mosaic decoration; the northern coast also has Cefalù, a seaside town with a magnificent Norman cathedral. Messina was destroyed in 1908 after an earthquake, and by the Allies in 1943. Taormina's classical remains, clinging to the cliffs beneath Mount Etna, are spectacular. And Agrigento's Temple of Concord is the best preserved Greek temple in Italy.

Sicily should be better known for its wine that it is now. It vies with Puglia for the title of the biggest wine producing area of Italy, and has an unimaginably large average annual output of about nine million hectolitres (roughly two hundred million gallons). Just to put this into an international context, this means that Sicily alone produces more wine than the whole of Australia.

There are nine Sicilian DOC wines including the much misunderstood Marsala, with all its variations. The

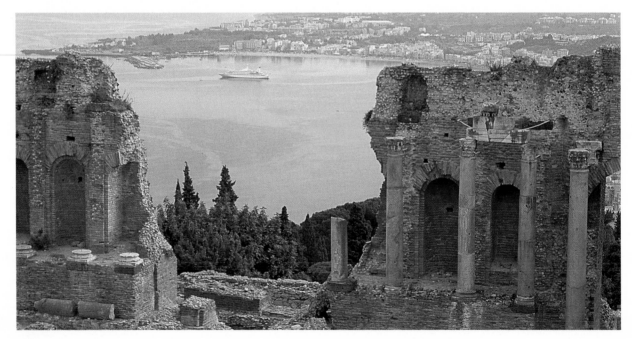

others are Bianco d'Alcamo, a white wine from the west of Sicily; Cerasuolo di Vittoria, a wine that is undergoing a renaissance of interest in the south of the island; Etna, from the slopes of the volcano; and Faro, from the north-east. Two delicious dessert wines, Malvasia delle Lipari and Moscato di Pantelleria, come from Sicily's islands; and finally, Moscato di Noto and Moscato di Siracusa exist on paper, but hardly at all in practice.

The most widely available and the most reliable wines are the big brands: Corvo (Duca di Salaparuta), Regaleali, Rapitalà, Donnafugata, Cellaro and Settesoli are the names to look for.

But there are some good smaller producers, too. COS, for example, who are leading the re-discovery of Cerasuolo di Vittoria, are fine wine producers at an international level.

There is plenty of potential in Sicily, but it has not been exploited yet.

PRINCIPAL VINEYARD AREAS

Marsala

Etna

Faro

Wines of Sicily

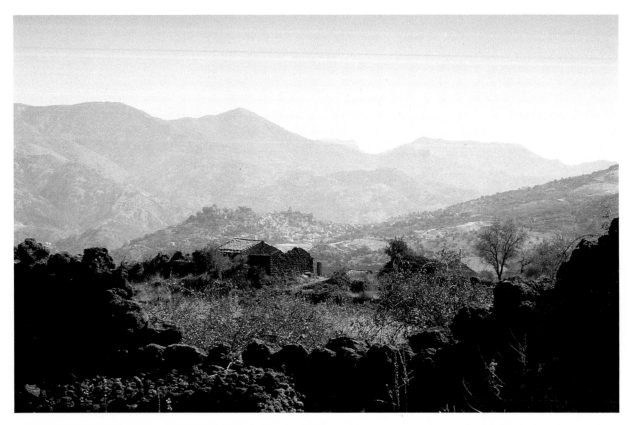

Dark volcanic soil around Mount Etna, whose lower slopes provide one of the island's most interesting DOC wines.

MILAZZO
Casa Vinicola Grasso*
Via Albero 5. Tel: 090 9281082. Fax: 090 9224001. (Alessio Grasso). 0800-1300, 1530-1930. Museum. T.F.WS. (B for groups.)

RAGUSA
Avide Corso Italia 131. Tel/Fax: 0932 967456. (Giuseppe Calcaterra). 0830-1700. E.T.F.WS.B.
Az Agr Coria Via Monreale 26. Tel/Fax: 0932 229229. Summer Tel/Fax: 0932 850022. (Giuseppe Coria). Own olive oil, honey. E.TP.WS.B.

Sicily can be divided into four for wine touring purposes: the north-east and east coast; the south-east and south coast; the west; and Pantelleria and the islands. Together with Lombardy, it shares the distinction of being the Italian beneficiary of a pan-European wine tourism project but, as yet, much is still in the planning stage.

Milazzo and Etna
Messina, the entry point to Sicily by car, was badly damaged in 1908 and 1943. But here the traveller has the choice of taking a ferry to the Aeolian islands and discovering the marvellous dessert wine from Lipari – Malvasia delle Lipari – or driving along the north coast to Milazzo, with its splendidly-sited 13th-century castle and the Grasso winery.

The third option is to head south on the A18 motorway to Taormina and Mount Etna. Scammacca and Villagrande are the two producers to visit in the area.

Etna has a legendary claim to be the first wine ever created. The young god Bacchus was walking to Sicily, when he stopped to rest on a tree stump, and a mysterious plant grew at his feet. He uprooted it and put it into the hollowed bone of a bird for safe keeping. As he journeyed, it grew so big that he put it in a lion's bone and finally in an ass's bone.

When he reached Nasso, near Taormina, he planted the vine, and it bore fruit. Bacchus picked the grapes and made the first wine. The story has a moral: a little wine makes you light like a bird, more of it makes you feel like a lion, immoderate use makes you an ass.

Pantelleria

Midway between Sicily and Tunisia is the beautiful island of Pantelleria. It can be reached by air, or by boat from Trapani, Mazara or Porto Empedocle on the Sicilian mainland. Its only main road is a picturesque coastal route.

In wine terms, this island, with its active volcanoes and hot springs, is disproportionately famous for its Moscato wine with its own romantic Greek legend. The goddess Thanit, enamoured of Apollo, substituted the wine of Pantelleria for his daily ambrosia, and immediately captured his attention. Indeed, it is the *passito* (sun-dried) grapes that produce the famous dessert Moscato, Passito di Pantelleria, which has discovered a ready export market. In a world looking for ever more variety in its wines, this is something different.

Moscato and Cerasuolo

Syracuse is the starting point for the third itinerary. The home of Plato and Archimedes, it is a potent reminder of the antiquity of civilization in Sicily. Certainly the city is more interesting from an historical point of view than its eponymous wine, Moscato di Siracusa, which is in any case almost impossible to find. The same applies to the other DOC Moscato of south-east Sicily; visit the town of Noto for its famous baroque architecture, but do not expect to find much Moscato di Noto wine.

The two Moscatos may lack convincing proponents; Cerasuolo di Vittoria, however, is one of the success stories of modern Sicilian viticulture. The name derives from its cherry-red colour, which makes it look like a dark rosé. In fact, the wine has good keeping qualities and, in the hands of producers such as COS, who were founded as recently as 1980

MILO
Az Agr Barone di Villagrande* Via del Bosco. Tel: 095 7894339. Fax: 095 7082175. (Carlo Nicolosi Asmundo). E.TP.WS.B.

S. VENERINA
Az Agr Emanuele Scammacca del Murgo Tenuta S Michele. Tel/Fax: 095 7130090. (Michele Scammacca del Murgo). F.TP.WS.B.

VITTORIA
Az Agr COS* Piazza del Popolo 34. Tel: 0932 864042. Fax: 0932 869700. (Giusto Occhipinti). E.F.TP.WS.B.

Moscato grapes laid out to dry in Pantelleria.

A market stall in Syracuse in south-east Sicily: shopping for fresh ingredients is a delight.

ACATE
Cantina Valle
dell'Acate* C.da Bidini.
Tel/Fax: 0932 874166.
(Gaetana Jacono). 0930-
1330, 1500-1730.
E.TF.WS.B.

VALLELUNGA
PRATAMENO
Conte Tasca
d'Almerita* Contrada
Regaleali. Tel: 0921
542522. Fax: 0921 542783.
(Giuseppe Tasca). 0800-
1300, 1400-1800.
E.TF.WS.B.

CALATAFIMI
Co-op Agr Marzuko*
Scalo Ferroviario. Tel/Fax:
0924 951191. (Francesco
Rotolo). 0800-1700.
Collection of agricultural
implements. E.TP.WS.B.

with the specific aim of re-
discovering the glories of Cerasuolo,
it is gaining a reputation as a fine
wine at an international level. There
is a *Strada del Vino* specifically for the
Vittoria area, bounded by the Ipari
and Dirillo rivers with the sea on one
side and the Iblei mountains on the
other.

Agrigento
The temples of Agrigento are a must,
but the modern town itself is worth
avoiding. Inland, at almost the dead
centre of the island, is one of Sicily's
top producers, Regaleali, a 300-
hectare (750 acre) estate owned by
the aristocratic Tasca d'Almerita
family.

Western Sicily
Most of the important wine
producers in Sicily, those with the
famous quality-conscious brands,
have their wineries in the north-
western part of Sicily. Rapitalà is
owned by the French count Hugues
de la Gatinais. Corvo is probably the
most successful brand; it is an
extremely reliable wine found all over
the world.

Donnafugata is an upmarket red
and white whose name comes from
the romantic *donna fugata*, 'the woman
who fled', a character in Giuseppe di
Lampedusa's novel *The Leopard*. The
princely villa in the story is on the
wine estate.

The making of Marsala
The story of Marsala dates back to
1773 when John Woodhouse, the son
of an English merchant from
Liverpool, was driven ashore at
Marsala by bad weather on one of
his usual trading trips to Italy. It
would not have been the first time he
had tasted Marsala, but he was sure
he could make a profit from shipping
it back to England. As was normal at
the time, a little spirit was added to
preserve the wine on its long voyage
back to England, exactly in the same
way as Port and Madeira were
transported.

Woodhouse's first shipment was of
50 pipes (412 litres each), but he
remained in the port of Marsala to
hear from his father in Liverpool
what he thought of the wine – the
response was enthusiastic and
Woodhouse set up in business.

The Woodhouse *Baglio*, or factory,
still stands by the shore in Marsala,
but much changed after two centuries
of export trade. Other Englishmen
soon followed Woodhouse.

Nelson's tipple

Originally there were three rival Marsala companies. Woodhouse's company and the wine were given official approval in 1798 when Nelson ordered his Marsala for the fleet after the battle of Aboukir Bay. He described the wine as 'good enough to be on the table of any gentleman'; the price was 5d (old pence) per gallon, freight-free to Malta. For a short time Marsala was referred to as 'Brontë-Madeira', after the title Duke of Brontë given to Nelson by the Bourbon government.

The other two companies were Ingham Whitaker & Co, founded by the Yorkshireman Benjamin Ingham in 1812, and Florio, founded by Vincenzo Florio in 1832. The busts of the three rivals are in the Florio museum, all three companies having been taken over by Cinzano before World War II.

Marsala and Garibaldi

Marsala can claim to have influenced the course of history. It was the presence of two English ships in the harbour that prevented the blockading Bourbon fleet from opening fire on Garibaldi as he landed with his famous Thousand volunteers in 1860.

Garibaldi's subsequent visit to the Florio Marsala winery led to a quality of Marsala being named after him; Garibaldi Dolce is still made today, and a plaque commemorating the visit is in the Florio museum.

Marsala today

The making of *zabaglione* would be impossible without Marsala. And that culinary necessity has kept the Marsala industry alive, sometimes to the detriment of its image. Until recently there was a danger that the real wine would become extinct, since it was disappearing into the sea of new mixed drinks; all sorts of versions were sold in the bottle – egg Marsala is perhaps the most notorious.

Marsala is, in fact, as versatile as sherry; it can be an aperitif or a digestif, it can be a fortified wine, or aged as a solera sherry.

Two other factors have saved it from extinction. Serious producers have realized that serious quality wines have to be made. Foremost among these is Marco de Bartoli, whose Vecchio Samperi is like an oloroso sherry, rich and nutty without being cloying. Secondly, a strict new code of Marsala production was introduced in 1984. Visit the Enoteca in Marsala for a tasting of modern Marsala.

Palermo is famous for its Baroque buildings and statuary, which includes the delightful 16th-century Pretoria Fountain.

MARSALA

Tenuta di Donnafugata* Via S Lipari 18. Tel: 0923 999555. Fax: 0923 721130. (Antonio Galassi). 0900-1230, 1500-1730. Historic cellars in Marsala dating back to 1851. E.F.G.TF.WS.B.

Cantine Florio Via Vincenzo Florio 1. Tel: 0923 781111. Fax: 0923 982380. (Signor Parisi). Mon-Thu 0900-1200, 1500-1700, Fri 0800-1200. Museum E.TF.WS. (B by fax).

Carlo Pellegrino & C.* Via del Fante 37. Tel: 0923 951177. Fax: 0923 953542. (Signor Catalano or Vito Cudia). 0830-1230, 1400-1730. E.F.TF.WS.B.

Az Ag Vecchio Samperi Contrada Fornara Samperi 292. Tel: 0923 962093. Fax: 0923 962510. Museum. E.F.TF.WS.B.

Sardinia

Sardinia is a very separate entity. The fashionable world may alight briefly at the Costa Smeralda on the north-eastern coast, but the Sardinians are still proudly insular, and lack the outward-going nature that gives other Italians of the South such a high profile. Instead, Sardinians are considered almost as mysterious as the neolithic *nuraghi* of their forefathers – round houses that you find throughout Sardinia that are constructed of enormous stones and used variously as fortresses, dwellings and watchtowers.

Viticulture in Sardinia has ancient traditions that go back as far as Phoenician times; these middle eastern traders of biblical times are credited with the introduction of the Nuragus grape to the island. The Spanish domination of Sardinia in the time of the Aragonese kingdom of Naples led to the introduction of Spanish grapes, Cannonau and Monica, in the 17th century. Sardinian agriculture gained most, however, from the period of the Savoy monarchy, in the 18th and 19th centuries, when immigrants from Piedmont, Liguria and Corsica brought with them new methods of wine-making, and new varieties of vine as well.

Table wines

On the whole, wine production in Sardinia is devoted to table wines of uncertain quality. There are some 39 co-operatives which account for 60 per cent of wine production, but only 4 per cent of all wine produced is DOC. There are few companies that export, and consequently few well known-Sardinian wines.

Producers

The most widely-available Sardinian wines come from the Sella & Mosca company in Alghero, on the north-western coast. They are a legacy of the Piedmontese interest in Sardinia; Emilio Sella and Edgardo Mosca were on a hunting holiday here in 1899 when they realized what ideal vine-growing country it was. Now Sella & Mosca is one of Europe's largest wine estates and a temple to modern technology. Their principal wines are the white Vermentino and Torbato and red Cannonau. The *barrique*-aged red Marchese di Villamarina has recently shown just how well Cabernet Sauvignon adapts to Sardinia.

Other wines and producers

Other producers of note include Attilio Contini with his long-lived Vernaccia di Oristano, and Argiolas, who produce a famous wine called Turriga. Of the co-operatives, the ones that stand out at the moment are Trexenta (honest Sardinian varietal wines), Santadi (currently regarded as the leader) and Jerzu (with its unique and highly alcoholic red wines).

Wine names to remember are: (reds) Cannonau, Monica di Sardegna, Carignano del Sulcis;

(whites) Malvasia, Moscato (a sweet dessert wine of the Càgliari district), Nuragus, Torbato, and Vernaccia di Oristano (similar to sherry; rich with a nutty aftertaste).

Sardinian food

The fundamental element in Sardinian food is bread. Bread is baked in a swallowtail shape for baptisms, in garlands for weddings, and brown bread underlines the sadness of funeral feasts.

The most famous product of the Sardinian bakery is *carta da musica*, 'music paper', paper-thin circular sheets of unleavened bread. Its origins lie in peasant cooking, when it was necessary for the shepherd to have something that would keep fresh on his long travels.

Another food of the Sardinian shepherd is cheese. *Cacio fiore* is the most traditional. It can be eaten fresh, grated, or aged with black pepper. Ricotta is called here *gentile*.

Cooking meat on a spit, flavoured with mint, rosemary, bay and sage, is traditional.

An alternative is *Carne a carraxiu*: sucking pig is encased in a sheep's stomach and covered with herbs. The parcel is placed in a hole in the ground full of embers and a fire is lit on top. *Porcheddu* is the dialect word for *porchetta*, roast sucking pig with rosemary.

Is malloredus are Sardinian *gnocchi* (tiny dumplings served as a first course), generally with a tomato or ragù sauce.

Fish is cooked simply. A speciality is the *bottarga* or *buttariga*, smoked mullet or tunny roe.

Sardinia vineyard areas

Grappa

CANELLI (Asti)
Distilleria Bocchino Via
G. B. Giuliani 88. Tel: 0141
8101. Fax: 0141 832547.
(Beppe Orsini). 0900-1200,
1500-1900. Museum, cellars
dug out of tufo rock.
T.P.WS.B.

**LIZZANO DI
ROVERETO (Trento)**
**Ernesto Barozzi
Distilleria Dante** Via
Isonzo 7. Tel: 0464 433713.
Fax: 0464 433713. (Signorina
Daniela). All year. TF. WS.

MONTEGALDA (Vicenza)
**Distilleria e Fabbrica
Liquori Fratelli Brunello**
Via Roi 27. Tel: 0444 636024.
Fax: 0444 636024. All year
(but pref. Sep-Nov). E.TF.WS.

**MUSOTTO D'ALBA
(Cuneo)**
Distilleria Santa Teresa
Case Sparse 35. Tel: 0173
33144. (Paolo Marolo).
Office hours. Max. 12
visitors at a time. E.F.TF.WS.

PERCOTO (Udine)
Distilleria Nonino Via
Aquileia 104. Tel: 0432
676333. Fax: 0432 676038.
(Signora Panelli). Office hours
Mon-Fri, Sat a.m. E.TF.WS.

PERGOLESE (Trentino)
Az Agr F.lli Pisoni Tel:
0461 56410. Fax: 0461
563163. (Marco or Elio
Pisoni). 0800-1200, 1330-
1830. Also wine producers.
E.G.WS.B.

SCHIAVON (Vicenza)
Distilleria G. B. Poli Via
G. Marconi 10. Tel: 0444
665007. Fax: 0444 665637.
(Jacopo Poli, Teresa Parma).
All year. Jacopo Poli is
founder of *Distillatori Artigiani
Vicentini* group of craftsmen/
distillers. E.F.TF.WS.

Among the many spirits and digestifs that come from Italy, grappa is one of the most maligned. Mention the equivalent French product, Marc de Bourgogne or Marc de Champagne, and there are instant smiles of recognition. But grappa, unfortunately, has a reputation as tourists' firewater. True, it can be undrinkable and in general it is wise to avoid anything that is very cheap. But it can also be a drink of the highest sophistication. Several different types are available. Grappa is produced throughout the hills and mountains of northern Italy and Tuscany. It is essentially the distillate of grape-pressings discarded by the wine-maker. Mobile stills used to be trundled from farm to farm at harvest time, transforming the waste of the wine-making process into a high-alcohol spirit, good for keeping the cold out in winter.

Today the traditional home-made grappa of the mountain farmer can still be found, served in the local trattorias in the Alps and the Dolomites. But modern grappa is usually the widely available brands, such as Grappa Julia and Carpenè Malvolti, sold in supermarkets, or the upmarket, luxury product served in smart restaurants.

Improvements in the techniques of vinification have also benefited the world of grappa. Top winemakers have begun to use free run juice for their wines, the result of soft pneumatic pressing. This leaves a much juicier and more flavoursome pomace for distillation.

Grappa technology has also improved in its own right. Many of the small distillers use discontinuous stills in a *bain marie*, or *bagna maria*, which allow the distillation to take place slowly and give the maximum flavour and sweetness. Logically enough, really fine grappa can only be made from fresh pomace, within 24 hours of the wine being drawn off the remains of the pressed grapes.

The best grappas are not technically grappas at all being the *distillato di uva*, a distillate of the whole grape, produced with the aim of making a spirit in the first place and never pressed for wine. (The result is technically an acquavit rather than a grappa.)

Grappa types

There are four types of grappa:
Grappa giovane This is young grappa, kept for about six months in stainless steel after distillation, thereby remaining clear in colour, and concentrating the natural tastes and fragrances of the distilled grapepressings.

Grappa invecchiata Aged grappa, kept for months or years in wood, which gives it an amber colour and makes it softer and smoother.

Grappa di monovitigno The most exclusive variety, made from a single grape variety in order to enhance its particular flavours. The strongly perfumed varieties are very attractive: Grappa di Moscato is a good example.

Grappa aromatizzata This is made with a herb or fruit flavouring and was traditionally used for medicinal purposes. Gentian-flavoured grappa, they say, is a remedy for insomnia. In Alto Adige, especially, there is a tradition of making fruit-flavoured Schnapps.

Grappa is the after-dinner drink of northern Italy and, after a recent revival, Tuscany. Producers can be visited in all those areas, but two in particular are outstanding.

The Nonino company, based in Friuli, were pioneers in the making of single-grape Grappas, the *Grappe di monovitigno* described above. Giannola Nonino saw the possibility of selecting a grape variety for its particular virtues of taste and fragrance. Some of Nonino's finest Grappas are aged in cherry wood, a practice that started because cherry trees are plentiful in the area. Now the single-grape, cherry-wood aged Grappas of Nonino in their bulbous bottles are amongst the most sought after in Italy.

In Piedmont, the Bocchino firm has made grappa for one hundred years.

Antonella Bocchino has rediscovered some of the traditional grape varieties of Piedmont to produce some very special single-grape Grappas. Neiret, Timuassa, Doux, and Vespolina d'Henry are some of the varieties. Visit the company in Canelli to see their unique museum of distillation. The Bocchino brand is a commercial grappa made from Moscato; Antonella's Grappas are much more expensive and are sold under the A.B. label.

Grappa is best drunk just slightly cool in small tulip-shaped glasses, in the best restaurants, of course. Older Italians are used to treating it with scant respect by putting a dash in their espresso coffee, the *caffè corretto*, or by mixing it with hot coffee in a wooden bowl with a lid and individual spouts, the *grolla* of the Aosta valley.

A grappa still in Piedmont. The art of distillation is a very ancient one, learned in part from the Arabs.

Reference Section

PRINCIPAL GRAPES AND THEIR WINES

Aglianico (red). Southern Italian grape of great antiquity. Its name derives from Hellenico, 'the Greek one'. It produces robust reds for long ageing in Basilicata (Aglianico del Vulture) and Campania (Taurasi).

Albana (white). Italy's first white DOCG is Albana di Romagna, made from this grape in central Italy. The wines are sweet or dry, still or sparkling.

Barbera (red). The staple grape of Piedmont, with Dolcetto. It makes intense reds for drinking within three years, such as Barbera d'Alba, d'Asti, del Monferrato.

Brunello (Sangiovese Grosso) (red). A type of Sangiovese used to make Italy's most prestigious wine, Brunello di Montalcino DOCG.

Cabernet Franc (red). Introduced to north-east Italy in the 19th century, this is widely used to make red wine with grassy characteristics.

Cabernet Sauvignon (red). One of the great grapes of the wine world. Hitherto only found on estates with francophile leanings: now widely planted as growers explore its undoubted potential.

Cannonau (red). This makes one of Sardinia's successful reds, Cannonau di Sardegna.

Chardonnay (white). One of the wine world's most fashionable grapes. Chardonnay from Burgundy produces rich and long-lived white wines. In Italy, it is not generally aged in the same way (in small oak barrels) to achieve the same intensity of flavour and length of ageing. Most Italian Chardonnay is fermented and aged in stainless steel, and therefore has a fresher taste.

Cortese (white). The grape used for Italy's most fashionable white, Gavi, and Cortese dei Colli Tortonesi, dell'Alto Monferrato, and di Gavi.

Corvina Veronese (red). One of the principal grapes of Valpolicella and Bardolino (together with Rondinella and Molinara).

Dolcetto (red). Piedmont's staple grape, along with Barbera. The name suggests sweetness, but it produces a smooth wine with a slightly bitter aftertaste, often used as a restaurant table wine.

Erbaluce (white). The Piedmontese grape, producing still, sparkling, dry and sweet wines.

Freisa (red). Still, sparkling, sweet or dry wines result from this grape with a characteristic strawberry aroma, from just south of Turin.

Gewürztraminer/Traminer Aromatico (white). Tramin/Termeno in Alto Adige claims to be the birthplace of this international grape. Used in north-east Italy.

Grechetto (white). The Umbrian grape that gives character to Orvieto.

Grignolino (red). This grape from the Asti region makes a light red/rosé wine with a slightly bitter aftertaste,

Lagrein (red). Produces a rosé (*kretzer*) or red (*dunkel*) wine in Alto Adige; light and drinkable wines.

Lambrusco (red). In Emilia Romagna, the wine from this grape is intended to cut the fatty foods of the region. The wine is usually dry, unlike the exported versions.

Malvasia (white). An ancient vine of possibly Greek origins. Malvasia di Candia is one of the major grapes of Frascati, Galestro, Est!Est!!Est!!! and Marino. It is also found extensively in Friuli-Venezia Giulia.

Marzemino (red). This makes a red wine from Trentino celebrated in Mozart's *Don Giovanni*.

Merlot (red). The workhorse grape of north-east Italy is now being re-evaluated as producers in Tuscany, Friuli and Alto Adige make prestigious wines from better clones.

Montepulciano (red). Used on the Adriatic coast to make the red wines Montepulciano d'Abruzzo and Rosso Conero. Not to be confused with the town of Montepulciano in Tuscany which has its own wine, Vino Nobile di Montepulciano made from the Sangiovese grape.

Moscato Bianco (white). One of the great grapes of Italy, this is the source of the fresh grapey tastes of Asti in Piedmont and Tuscany's Moscadello di Montalcino.

Müller-Thurgau (white). An international grape variety giving a sophisticated but fruity white wine mostly in Friuli-Venezia Giulia and Trentino-Alto Adige.

Nebbiolo (red). The source of two of Italy's best-known and longest-lived wines, Barolo and Barbaresco. Also the base grape for several northwestern Italian reds.

Negroamaro (red). Puglia's most important grape.

Picolit (white). The legendary dessert wine of Friuli, Picolit, is made from the semi-dried grapes of the same name. It is high in alcohol and can be aged for several years.

Pinot Bianco (white). Often confused with Chardonnay by the growers, this grape gives a similar taste to wines mainly made in Friuli and Trentino-Alto Adige.

Pinot Grigio (red). The grape's red skins often give its white wines an attractive pink tinge. The wine has become popular as the thinking skier's white wine. It has good body with a characteristic aromatic twist.

Pinot Nero (red). The best reds of Burgundy are produced from this difficult grape, which has inspired producers in north-east Italy and Tuscany to attempt to do likewise.

Prosecco (white). Versatile grape of the Treviso area of the Veneto. Most popular for the medium dry sparkling wine that is Treviso's house wine.

Riesling (white). The native Italico is less pungent than the Germanic Riesling Renano. Mainly used for varietals in north-east Italy.

Sagrantino (red). An indigenous grape in Umbria, used for red wines with aromas of blackberries and mushrooms.

Sangiovese (red). One of Italy's finest grapes, used in its various forms throughout Central Italy for wines such as Chianti, Vino Nobile di Montepulciano, Brunello and Carmignano (Tuscany), and Rosso Piceno (the Marches).

Sauvignon (white). The grassy green-stick bouquet and flavour of this international grape is less aggressive in Italy than in France.

Schiava/Vernatsch (red). The base grape of the red wines of Trentino Alto Adige, such as Santa Maddalena, Caldaro and Casteller.

Sylvaner (white). Better known in Alsace, this is also used in Alto Adige to make aromatic white wines.

Tocai Friulano (white). The most common white grape of the eastern Veneto and Friuli-Venezia Giulia.

Trebbiano (white). The grape responsible for most of Italy's white wines, especially Soave, Gambellara, and Frascati.

Verdicchio (white). The versatile white wine grape of the Marches area. It makes still or sparkling wine and can also be aged in small casks.

Verduzzo (white). Produces a white dessert wine from Friuli capable of being aged in *barriques*.

Vernaccia di San Gimignano (white). Responsible for San Gimignano's white wine.

GLOSSARY OF WINE TERMS

Abboccato Slightly sweet; Orvieto Abboccato is the most typical.
Acciaio (or **Inox**) Stainless steel
Affinamento Ageing (after fermentation, in barrel or in bottle).
Amabile Sweet.
Autoclave The tank in which sparkling wine made by the Charmat method (*Metodo Charmat*) gets its sparkle.
Barrique Small, new oak barrel, now fashionable in Italy. Its use gives a smooth, initially vanilla, flavour.
Bianco White.
Bicchiere Glass.
Botte Large barrel, usually made from Slavonian oak

Bouquet Smell of the wine, resulting from grape, vinification and ageing.
Brillante Very clear.
Brut Very dry, applied to sparkling wines.
Cantina Cellar.
Castagno Chestnut wood.
Corpo Body and structure of a wine.
Cru Single vineyard.
Da bere fresco To be drunk cool.
Degustazione A tasting, the occasion for the **assaggio** (process of tasting).
Dolce Very sweet.
Equilibrato Balanced.
Erbaceo Grassy, especially applicable to Cabernet Franc.
Etichetta Label.
Fermentazione Fermentation.
Frizzante Slightly sparkling.
Fruttato Fruity.
Giallo paglierino Straw yellow.
Giovane Young.
Gradevole Attractive to drink.
Invecchiamento Process of ageing.
Liquoroso Wine fortified with added alcohol, such as Marsala.
Millesimato Vintage wine.
Morbido Smooth and soft.
Neutro Without characteristics.
Ossidazione Oxidization.
Ossigenazione The process of letting wine breathe, especially desirable for older red wines.
Passito A rich wine high in alcohol, such as Recioto, from semi-dried grapes.
Pieno Full, as in full of flavour.
Pigiatura Pressing, the first process of wine-making.
Pronta beva To be drunk soon after bottling.
Resa Yield (of grapes per plant or per hectare/acre).

139

Retrogusto Aftertaste.
Robusto A big wine, full of colour, acidity, alcohol and tannin.
Rosato Rosé.
Rosso Red.
Rotondo Smooth.
Rovere Oak.
Rubino Ruby red.
Sapido Full of taste.
Secco Dry.
Spumante Sparkling wine. The sparkle can be produced by the *Metodo Champenois* or the *Método*

Charmat (see above), or by artificially adding bubbles.
Tannico Tannin; in a red wine this indicates that it will age well.
Tappo The cork. The same word means 'corked', that is, with a bitter taste given to the wine by a bad cork.
Tastevin Small silver tasting bowl used instead of a glass in the cellar.
Tipicità 'Typicality', meaning the wine is authentic and traditional.
Torchio Old-fashioned wine press.

Uva Grape.
Uvaggio Proportional blend of grapes, *cépage*.
Vellutato Smooth, velvety.
Vendemmia Vintage, harvest.
Vigna, vigneto Single vineyard.
Vignaiolo Grower of grapes.
Vinificazione Vinification.
Vinoso 'Like wine', term used especially of a characterless bouquet.
Vivace Fresh and often slightly sparkling.

RED WINES FOR LAYING DOWN, 1970-95

	Barbaresco	Brunello di Montalcino	Barolo	Chianti Classico	Vino Nobile di Montepulciano	Amarone
1970	••••	••••	••••	•••••	••••	••••
1971	••••	•••	•••••	•••••	••••	••••
1972	•	•	•	••	•	•
1973	••	•••	••	••	•••	••
1974	••••	••	••••	•••	•••	••••
1975	••	•••••	••	•••••		•••
1976	••	•	••	••	••	••••
1977	••	••••	••	••••	••••	•••
1978	•••••	••••	•••••	•••••	•••••	•••
1979	••••	••••	••••	••••	••••	••••
1980	••••	••••	••••	••••	••	•••
1981	•••	•••	•••	•••	•••	•••
1982	•••••	•••••	•••••	••••	••••	•
1983	••••	••••	••••	••••	••••	•••••
1984	•	••	••	•	•	••
1985	•••••	•••••	•••••	•••••	•••••	••••
1986	•••	•••	•••	••••	••••	•••
1987	••	••	••	••	••	••
1988	•••••	•••••	•••••	•••••	•••••	•••••
1989	•••••	••	•••••	•	•	••
1990	•••••	•••••	•••••	•••••	•••••	•••••
1991	•••	•••	•••	•••	•••	••
1992	••	••	••	•	•	•
1993	•••	••••	•••	••••	•••••	••••
1994	••	••	••	••	••	••
1995	••••	•••••	••••	••••	••••	••••

Key to vintage wine chart
Vintages are assessed with star ratings. Five stars indicate an exceptionally good vintage. Remember that vintage wines need several years' ageing in barrel and in bottle before they are released on to the market.

SAMPLE LETTER TO AN ITALIAN WINERY

[Sender's name, address and telephone number; date]

La presente per chiedere la prenotazione di una nostra visita alla Vostra stimata cantina.

Abbiamo sentito la fama dei Vostri vini tramite il libro A Traveller's Wine Guide to Italy, nel quale si nota la Vostra gentile disponibilità a dare ai viaggiatori intenditori una visita/degustazione alla cantina. Perciò, siccome siamo molto interessati a sapere di più sul vino italiano in genere e sul Vostro vino in particolare saremmo molto interessati ad approfittare dell'occasione.

Siamo un piccolo gruppo di [X] persone. Abbiamo intenzione di visitare la Vostra zona i giorni [dates] e chiediamo la Vostra gentile conferma della disponibilità di accoglierci.

Nell'attesa del piacere della Vostra cortese risposta e del piacere dell' eventuale incontro porgiamo i nostri più cordiali saluti,

[Signature]

We would like to arrange a visit to your excellent Cantina.

We have heard of the fame of your wines through the publication *A Traveller's Wine Guide to Italy*, from which we understand that you are willing to accept visits from travellers who are wine lovers and who wish to taste wine in your cellars. We are very interested in learning more about Italian wine in general, and about your wine in particular.

We are a small group of [X] people. We intend to visit your area on the following dates [***] and would be very pleased if you could confirm that you would be able to accept a visit on one of those days.

We look forward to your reply and to the pleasure of meeting you when this can be arranged.

With best wishes,

[Signature]

FURTHER READING

(In English)

Burton Anderson, *The Wine Atlas of Italy*. From a technical point of view, the best book on Italian wines currently available.

Burton Anderson, *Vino*. A standard work on Italian wines, by the leading English-language writer on the subject.

Burton Anderson, *The Pocket Guide to Italian Wine*.

Nicolas Belfrage, *Life Beyond Lambrusco*. In-depth examination of the current state of wine-making in Italy.

David Gleave, *The Wines of Italy*. Well-illustrated guide to Italian wine by grape variety.

Marc and Kim Millon, *The Wine Roads of Italy*. Itineraries through most major wine-producing areas.

Bruno Roncarati, *Viva Vino*. A useful reference work.

Sheldon and Pauline, Wasserman *Italy's Noble Red Wines*. Comprehensive tasting notes on a wide range of the finer Italian reds.

(In Italian)

Guida all'Italia dei Vini (Touring Club Italiano, 1985) Geographic guide to Italian DOCs and DOCGs.

Marco Trimani, *Guida ai Vini d'Italia* (Editori Riuniti, 1984). A basic dictionary of Italian wine, with notes on vinification.

Luigi Veronelli, *Le Cantine di Veronelli* (Giorgio Mondadori, 1989). Recommended wine producers with details of which wines to taste on a visit and how to book that visit.

ITALIAN NATIONAL HOLIDAYS

January 1: New Year
January 6: Epiphany
Easter Monday: (dates vary)
April 25: Liberation Day.
May 1: Labour Day.
August 15: Assumption of the Virgin.
November 1: All Saints Day.
December 8: Feast of the Immaculate Conception.
Christmas Day and Boxing Day.

Local feast days

Shops and businesses are often closed during festivities. The following is a selection only:
April 25: Venice.
June 24: Florence. Genoa. Turin
June 29: Rome.
July 15: Palermo.
September 19: Naples.
October 4: Bologna.
December 6: Bari.
December 7: Milan.

Index

Page numbers in *italic* type indicate illustrations.